Poems for a Century

Poems for a Century

An Anthology on Nigeria

Edited by
Tope Omoniyi

AMALION
PUBLISHING

Published by Amalion Publishing 2014

Amalion Publishing
BP 5637 Dakar-Fann
Dakar CP 00004
Senegal
http://www.amalion.net

ISBN 978-2-35926-032-8 (Paperback)
ISBN 978-2-35926-033-5 (EPub)
ISBN 978-2-35926-040-3 (Kindle)

Cover illustration *Ekuoregbe IV* by Bruce Onobrakpeya, courtesy
of the artist

Cover designed by Anke Rosenlöcher

Contents

Foreword

On the occasion of the formal amalgamation of the two Nigerias I wish you to convey to the emirs, chiefs, and all the inhabitants of the new Protectorate and the Colony my best wishes for their future happiness. Pray assure them of the great interest I take in all that concerns their welfare and express my earnest hope that great prosperity may be in store for them. — GEORGE R.I. (An extract of a telegram from His Majesty the King to Sir Frederick Lugard, Governor-General of Nigeria, sent December 30, 1913)[1]

The word 'Nigeria' was first used in print in an article written by Flora Shaw, published in *The Times* of January 8, 1897, without the author's name in the then tradition of the paper. In it, the author, who had been a foreign correspondent and expert on colonial territories for the paper for a couple of years previously, fleshed out the importance of the diverse geographical configurations under the British through her Royal Niger Company, and more importantly foreshadowed the administrative modus operandi that would culminate in the creation of a single entity called Nigeria in 1914. Shaw, a published novelist and children's book author in earlier times, argued for this name:

> In the first place, as the title "Royal Niger Company's Territories" is not only inconvenient to use but to some extent is also misleading, it may be permissible to coin a shorter title for the agglomeration of pagan and Mohammedan states which have been brought, by the exertions of the Royal Niger Company, within the confines of the British Protectorates, and thus need for the first time in their history to be described as an entity by some general name. To speak of them as the Central Sudan, which is the title accorded by some geographers and travellers, has the disadvantage of ignoring political frontier-lines, while the word "Sudan" is too apt to connect itself in the public mind as the French *Hinterland of Algeria*, or the vexed questions of the Niger basin. The name "Nigeria", applying to no other portion of Africa, may, without offence to any neighbours, be accepted as coextensive with the territories over

---

1   "United Nigeria, His Majesty's Telegram to the Governor", *The Times,* January 3, 1914, page 7.

which the Royal Niger Company has extended British influence, and may serve to differentiate them equally from the British colonies of Lagos and the Niger Protectorate on the coast and from the French territory of the Upper Niger. [2]

According to AHM Kirk-Greene, however, the adjective "Nigerian" had been used by W. Cole in his *Journal of an African Trader, or Life in the Niger, 1859–60*, but its connotation was solely of the Lower Niger basin".[3] Until Flora Shaw's use of the term "Nigeria" in 1897, several other names used to describe the geographical area included "Hausa Territories", the "Niger Empire", "Niger Soudan", in addition to the regional titles of "Royal Niger Company's Territories," "Niger Coast Protectorate" and "Oil Rivers" amongst others. Names fashioned and changed as the British configured and reconfigured its territories acquired through what Shaw euphemistically termed 'exertions' of the Royal Niger Company (RNC). Large sections of the territories in question were actually bought by the British Government from the RNC, whose charter was about to expire by 1900. The brutal force and phony treaties that the RNC used to 'acquire' the territories in the first place are well documented in the annals of history, but not the focus of this foreword.

In the 1897 piece, and in subsequent presentations[4], articles and a book, Flora Shaw not only expounded on a mercantile and racist civilizing mission and the need to quickly bring all their 'tropical responsibilities' or 'dependencies' into a single administration, but also explicitly prepared the ground for pitting specific indigenous groups against others that would impact on the politics of the country till today. Flora Shaw was no ordinary hack; apart from her colonial journalistic explorations to various places including Australia, Canada, South Africa and the Belgian Congo, by 1902

---

2 "Nigeria", *The Times*, January 8, 1897, page 6. See also "Flora Shaw gives the name", *The Times*, September 30, 1960.

3 "Nigeria and 'The Times'", *The Times British Colony Reviews*, Second Quarter 1959, page 3.

4 Lady Lugard on Nigeria, *The Times*, March 2, 1904; *A Tropical Dependency*, 1905.

she was married to Sir Frederick Lugard, High Commissioner for Northern Nigeria and later Governor-General of the two protectorates of Northern and Southern Nigeria and of the ultimate formal unified Colony and Protectorate of Nigeria in January 1914. If the couple were already dating by 1897 could be of tabloid interest if some Late Victorian muck could be dug up. What is clear is that Lugard's role in the construction of British colonial administration makes this couple a formidable duo in the history of Nigeria and its nearly one million square kilometres and estimated 170 million people.

A hundred years after unification, the most populous African and biggest black nation on earth has oscillated from being great to being fickle, from colony to independence and dependency, from peace to war to ungraceful insecurity, military dictatorship to civilian oppression and profligacy and much more of the many contradictions of a complex national polity. The nation is a hundred years old and yet a 'half-child' to borrow Ogaga Ifowodo's metaphor.

Its peoples have even tried to change the name, albeit in mindset and beer parlour and motor park settings. 'Nigeria' is what's on the 'green passport' that gets you 'extra scrutiny and harassment'[5] on a waiting line at an airport, it also conjures the Olympic football winning team and the Nobel prize author, and the big spending African brother whose charities do not always start at the homestead. 'Naija' on the hand is something special. It is all of the above plus a unique dynamism against all odds, where nothing is impossible. It is Nairobi-kids bred on Nollywood and P-Square speaking in Nigerian accent. It is the always feel good factor that make you park a Mercedes-Benz side by side the open sewage in front of your house. It is the perpetual oil subsidy removal and fuel scarcity in one of the world's largest oil-exporting countries. It is irrepressible Fela Anikulapo Kuti and an acerbic tongue and irresistible dance beats. This special collection *Poems for a Century*

---

5   Opening sequence to the documentary 'Naij: A History of Nigeria', by Jide Olanrewaju, 2007. Actualize Production.

is to mark whichever feeling of celebration or oppression that that name 'Nigeria' or the feeling of being 'Naija' evokes.

In the Introduction, Tope Omoniyi explains the roots of the project, which began from the caution for celebration of suffering in the midst of plenty after over half a century of independence, to the need to note the centenary anniversary of the country's amalgamation. This amalgamation has critical impact on the social political structure and framework of the entity that became independent in 1960. To imagine what and how the country's past and present would have been shaped is not just an exercise in historiography. Each political economic crisis, each pipeline leak and blast, each martial music announcement, and each corruption scandal have ensured that Nigerians continue to ponder on this question daily, proffering and refuting panaceas to satisfy interests at shifting circumstances and positions. That the discourse often deliberately obfuscate or side step whatever benefits such an amalgamation have brought on Nigeria is moot in a nation whose majority citizens cannot fathom why the country is so rich and their lives so poor. A nation where to be 'oppressed' is to bear daily witness to the stupendous wealth of other Nigerians side by side your own harsh penury. A country best described by Dagga Tolar in a scathing cry for social justice:

> The colour of this country is not black, is not white
> Like in the colour of skins
> This country celebrates its colour
> Not in the colourless of water
> But in the colourful colour of unclean water
> That too many people get to drink and die.[6]

Omoniyi's introduction provides an interesting analysis on the characteristics and thematic preoccupations of the poets in this collection and the role of the artist in the community. He raises the contextual roots of the motivations of some Nigerian poets and writers and the impact of generational and intergenerational

---

6   Extract from "This country dying undead" by AJ Dagga Tolar, 2011.

discourse in situating this collection. This foreword aims to raise additional issues around the creative artform of poetry in Nigeria and its impact on the question of nationhood in the country.

That the poems in the collection were specifically chosen because they were written about the Nigerian question and condition is of no doubt, hence the similarity in thematic preoccupation. This similarity however is more telling of contemporary poetry in Nigeria than beyond an anniversary collection. The writer Sule E. Egya, who has a contribution in this collection, in his essay "Art and Outrage,[7] eloquently reviews the traditions and social context of Nigerian poets and their contributions to map out the specific features of poetry in the country today. He argues that a megatheme of commitment to the lot of the nation runs through the work of the majority of Nigerian poets in English, constituting a 'discourse of grief, personal, communal and nationalistic'[8] that runs across generations from Christopher Okigbo to Niyi Osundare. He concludes: 'The nation as an imagined community, and its internal disruptions by powerful forces and the avowed determination of the poets to engage the disruptions, has powered the vision of this poetry.' Metaphors of bleakness, anguish, and frustration become essential signifiers of a dirge-like poetry constituting what Pius Adesanmi also aptly referred to as an 'aesthetics of pain'[9].

To come away with the view that poetry in Nigeria is all *engagé* misses the point, as some of the lines in this collection will attest. Even as the senses of helplessness cut across generations, Nigerians over the years have utterly complex relationships with how they perceive joy and suffering and situate responsibility for the nation's polity. For instance, as more Nigerians are being born with fading or no memory of martial music on the radio, the understanding of the military and militarisation in Nigeria may be

7   "Art and Outrage: A Critical Survey of Recent Nigerian Poetry in English", *Research in African Lit*, Vol., 42, no 1, 2011, pp 49–67.

8   Ibid: p. 64.

9   Adesanmi, Pius. "Europhonism, Universities, and Other Stories: How Not to Speak for the Future of African Literatures." *Palavers of African Literature: Essays in Honor of Bernth Lindfors*, Vol. 1. Ed. Toyin Falola and Barbara Harlow. Trenton: AWP, 2002. 105-136.

perplexing across generations. For its Generation 2.0, suffering is being deprived of a facebook or twitter account. Or some of us just want to watch football leagues and express ferocious loyalty to clubs from afar, as Jekwu Ozoemene mocks in 'Our beautiful game'.

Dissemination remains a critical factor in being able to spread an avowedly political message for Nigerian poets. Traditions of modern poetry have never been the most public of the literary art-forms in Nigeria. If the desire is to reach a critical mass to stir a revolution, other literary and cultural artforms might be better suited. Oral poetry forms in indigenous languages have had much better success. Poetry in English in a country such as Nigeria is already limited as it were that the number of poetry books sold or shared will pale in comparison with the readers of novels and theatre goers or home video viewers for instance. Yet Nigerian poets in English have continued to strive to publish in what has been a difficult publishing environment, particularly in the 1980s and 1990s with a devalued naira and highly inflationary economic terrain.

On one level, the public and readership have not been mainly local. Migration and diaspora tenterhooks have added new spaces for readership as well as publishing. On another level, the internet and social media have provided a platform in recent years that was not available to writers two decades ago. Poets now have a chance to go beyond restricted groups and exclusive literary fraternities. Blog websites and facebook pages are replete with new verses for both critical appreciation and popular enjoyment. The oft-repeated excuse of the reluctant publisher of poetry seems to be gaining less weight for serious writers interested in the craft.

The reality of this age however is that getting that critical mention is becoming more difficult in the deluge of verses and words floating in cyberspace. Self-publishing is becoming less an answer to solve this than ever. Apart from limited editorial capacities and subsequent amplified embarrassment in some situations[10], the network needed to build a writer, to take them to the next level of their craft and bring their message and their art to the attention of a wider audience beyond theirs, can barely be accomplished effectively by self-publishing poetry.

At Amalion, the need for us to publish poetry can barely be linked to the direct ROI on a particular poet or title. We may hope to break even but even this get tempered swiftly by the obvious reality that there are so many poets out there who they themselves do not buy poetry books either occasionally or regularly! Not surprisingly, many a glorious turn of phrase and sonorous alliterative lines does not a publishing business float. And if you work in the mindset of the 'Incentivised Generation', with the hope to win an 'award', pray your electricity, phone and internet access are still running by the time that lucky email lands.

Omoniyi is so true when he notes that poetry is about capturing moments in the lives of people and nations. Like other artforms it is a mirror to both the social context of our world and a connection to the dreams of our future and much more. To publish poetry is to gather, albeit curate, the unending possibilities of language in use and much more. To publish the poetry of writers from Senegal, Uganda, Nigeria, and other parts of Africa is to keep the tradition of an artform critical to building writers in other literary genres. The condensed discipline inculcated in a poet when put to good use in other literary forms moves language into another realm of human feeling and thought. Percy Bysshe Shelley goes further,

> Poetry enlarges the circumference of the imagination by replenishing it with thoughts of ever new delight, which have the power of attracting and assimilating to their own nature all other thoughts, and which form new intervals and interstices whose void forever craves fresh food. Poetry strengthens the faculty which is the

---

10 The LNG Prize for Literature, the largest literary award prize in the country and continent, worth a 100,000 dollars, raised controversy when its judges claimed, no book was worth the prize in 2004 as all submissions were replete with editorial errors.

organ of the moral nature of man, in the same manner as exercise strengthens a limb. [11]

In the coming years we hope we can do more than publish poets from Africa. We hope we can be able to open spaces of engagement for African writers beyond their imagination and experiences. Paul Celan's thought of poets gathering their words in a bottle to toss into sea for someone somewhere to discover and own[12] soothes some of the hard knocks of our publishing lives.

A poem, as a manifestation of language and thus essentially dialogue, can be a message in a bottle, sent out in the — not always greatly hopeful — belief that somewhere and sometime it could wash up on land, on heartland perhaps. Poems in this sense, too, are under way: they are making toward something.

We are excited about our involvement with the African Poetry Book Fund and Series set up by Kwame Dawes to promote the writing and publication of African poetry through an international complex of collaborations and partnerships. Starting in March 2014, the Series will publish four new titles by African poets each year and an anthology every few years representing themes, ideas and poets from across the African continent. Of the four books to be published, by the University of Nebraska Press and Amalion Publishing, one will be a winner of the Sillerman First Book Prize for African Poets, and a second will be a new and selected volume by a major African poet. The Fund and its partners aim to offer support for seminars, workshops, and other publishing opportunities for African poets.

We would like to thank all the contributors in the volume and a special thank you to Tope Omoniyi for putting this collection together and for proposing that Amalion be the publisher of such an august collection in the history of Nigeria. Big thank you to Chief Bruce Onobrakpeya for his kind permission to use his artwork on the cover. The diversity and breadth of the contributors

---

11 Percy Bysshe Shelley, A Defence of Poetry (1821), http://www.poetryfoundation.org/learning/essay/237844?page=3

12 Paul Celan, cited in 'Heartland' by Edward Hirsch, available at http://www.poetryfoundation.org/learning/article/177205,

and contributions truly attest to the plurality of the complex scape otherwise known as Nigeria. That the poets come from different careers and backgrounds and parts of the country, flung and dispersed in different corners of the country and globe, is beyond an exercise in 'federal character', it rather reminds us in some way that caution is necessary to interpret this or any other anthology exercise prescriptively. Yes, it is a take, a valid sample of the varied tastes and myriad expressions of poetry and poets drawing on the muse Nigeria today.

—Sulaiman Adebowale

Introduction

I shall begin with a disclaimer. It is neither my objective as editor of this festive anthology to capture and reflect the state of Nigerian poetry today nor is it my desire to represent the work of the 'Who is who' of poetry in the country. Both of those aims I believe are the exclusive challenge of those who over the years have earned the nomenclature of critical watchers of Nigerian poetry writing. I do not belong in that category. I am one of a tribe of verse-men and verse-women thrown out with the bathwater by successive pariah regimes during the intellectual haemorrhage of the 1980s and early 1990s. For some of us in this group, the clinicians of Dodan Barracks did not sever the umbilical cord completely and in the intervening years its regrowth has become the return pathway to the Mother Ship for troubadours.

What then is my objective? Poetry is about capturing moments. Poetry is a moment perceived, constructed and preserved in verse by a poet. The moment may be now as is often the case or one located in a past that is the subject of present reflective thinking, recollection, reprocessing and repackaging in relation to current development or circumstance. The idea of a poetry anthology to mark a nation's independence anniversary at first sounded a little strange. It is not the result of a project long deliberated upon. In fact, one of the immediate problems I confronted was in recruiting the desired number of contributors due to the time limitation of the schedule. In spite of this problem and as daunting as it seemed, I must concede that my final push was more anger than literary. It was the raging debate in the Nigerian media of the commitment of a staggering sum of N10 billion in a supplementary budget submitted to the National Assembly for a celebration of the independence anniversary of 2010. The Nigerian Labour Congress described it as 'lavish' and 'wasteful', advising the government instead to direct "energies and national resources towards entrenching democratic cultures and values in the hearts of our people and in our institutions in order to redeem our lost glory and dignity." (Sanni Ologun, *The Nation*, June 8, 2010).

This call to celebrate the national moment in ways more sensitive to the realities of "national gloom, due obviously to our stunted growth in many aspects of our political economy"[13] and a global economy in disarray, constituted a framework within which energies, national resources, cultures, values, lost glory and dignity needed to be problematized in order to review, imagine, and re-envision the Nigerian nation. The thought of the intense emotions that compatriots felt and expressed about nationhood in 2010 presented a unique and peculiar vantage moment from which to challenge poets to participate in this project. In a country where the average lifespan is officially put at 52, fifty becomes either a landmark celebration or a moment for sober reflection. In my primary constituency the academy, it is about the earliest age at which some lucky bastards have earned a festschrift by a collection of those who hold them in high esteem. Among global institutions, half a century is in the same category as a decade, quarter century and century in the demarcation of review periods. So, beyond capturing the moment of 50 this volume is also in part intended to present a multiple perspective review of the period in question in verse. In reality, however, this period cannot be taken completely out of context. The nation 'Nigeria' officially started in 1914 when several geographical blocs were amalgamated for effective colonial administration. That the volume is being released during the centenary year is deliberately fortuitous so to speak.

Adaobi Tricia Nwaubani writing in the *New York Times* of December 11, 2010 chastised African writers for modelling their writing on Africa's most acclaimed writers Wole Soyinka and Chinua Achebe. She says inter alia,

> Here, each successful seller of plantain chips spawns a thousand imitators selling identical chips; conformity is esteemed while individuality raises eyebrows; success is measured by how similar you are to those who have gone before you. These are probably not uniquely African flaws, but their effects are magnified on a continent whose floundering publishing industry has little money for

---

13 'N10 billlion for nation's Golden Jubilee wasteful, says NLC', *Vanguard*, June 7, 2010.

experimentation and whose writers still have to move abroad to gain international recognition.

The logic is a simple one I dare suggest. As the Yoruba say *ęsin iwaju ni t'ęhin nwo s'aré* and it is sheer folly to change a winning formula especially written literature in English. In the tradition of early Nigerian poetry in English, JP Clark, Wole Soyinka, Gabriel Okara, and Christopher Okigbo represent a phase of enhancement marked by complex and not easy to decipher content. Arguably, the problem in sticking with these poetic models of course is a creative hamstring that challenges originality of form and style. Consequently, the citation will often go to the original rhythm masters. The next generation was marked by a seeming rejection of any form of imposition, and the adoption of a fiercer spirited approach that was marked by bravado in experimenting with new content and forms. Lyricism and rhythm had an edge over rhyme. They explored polyphony, collective sentiments, sensibilities and destinies. To this category belong Tanure Ojaide, Niyi Osundare, Odia Ofeimun, Harry Garuba and a number of others. Indigenous ritual practices, languages, and knowledge generally were legitimised and celebrated. Poetry added an entertainment dimension to its critical purpose.

The tradition of exploring local cultures and epistemology continued in what has become known as the Third Generation of poets whom I prefer to refer to as the Poetry Workshop Generation of the 1980s across Nigerian university campuses. Those workshops were the factory floors on which the writers honed their art into literary warheads against the military dictatorships and big garment contract regimes of the day to force social change. They include among others Remi Raji, Uche Nduka, Onookome Okome, and Ogaga Ifowodo. Out of the University of Lagos, I ran the Ijiomi Poetry Club which counted among its membership Hope Eghagha, Cyril Obi and our late friend Esiri Dafiewhare. The highlight of our year was the May 1st Celebration of Life. In terms of publishing, arguably Harry Garuba's Malthouse anthology *Voices from the Fringe: An ANA Anthology of New Nigerian Poetry* (1988) remains the flagship publication of that era. I remember our own attempts to get Longman interested in individually authored poetry volumes and their attempts to convert us to contributors to the Drumbeats fiction series they had just set up.

Since the Workshop Generation, the Association of Nigerian Authors (ANA) and new literary prize funders like NLNG and the Okigbo Prize, established by Soyinka, have given fresh impetus to Nigerian poetry and poets. Perhaps if one were crazed about compartmentalizing Nigerian poets at all costs, then this could be said to have created one other category – the "Incentivised Generation" for whom poetry became imagined as a liberator. In the harsh economic climate of the 1990s two types of writers emerged, those who came to poetry as a means to the end of winning the various pots of gold prizes and those who saw the prizes as testimony to peer recognition and acceptance of their craft and possibly a promise that they could partially view writing both as art and as a means of livelihood. In addition to the major annual prizes, there were the occasional one-off prizes which were directed at specific events. In 1985, the Federal Ministry of Information organised the National Anti-Apartheid Poetry Competition. I remember that as joint winner of the runner-up prize with Tade Akin Aina I received a clock which to this day continues to tick even after Baba to whom I proudly gave it as a mark of filial devotion ceased ticking (June 12, 2010).

Finally, I wish to end with a short commentary on the line-up of poets in this anthology. Although the poets have all engaged with Nigeria from differing perspectives and positions, there is no doubt that the nation is organic and therefore that a poetic relay ensures the continuity of our vision. In the light of that fact, the anthology is dedicated as it were to two groups of compatriots, those whose journeys with the Nigerian nation either came to an end or commenced in 2010. This is important because between them they bridge the nation's past, present and future.

An overview of the poems

There are 50 poems in all in this volume to mark Nigeria's fiftieth independence anniversary. Thus there's a natural thematic spine to the volume but anchorage to this spine varies from one poem to another, some more so than others. In other words some poems expressly celebrate turning fifty and what it means for Nigeria as a nation or what characterises the attainment of that age in nationhood. Tade Akin Aina's poem 'How do we sing a song to fifty years in dependence?' questions the fact and integrity of Nigeria's independence through a play on the word itself evoking images of grimness and the seriousness of the challenge that confronts those who believe in and are committed to the Nigerian state as one indivisible entity. A sentiment of hope is conveyed in several other poems in the same category, Okinba Launko's 'A song for a mother's birthday' and Tolu Ogunlesi's 'Nigerian dream' and Ismail Bala's 'After the lean harvest, Lord it's time' exemplify this richly.

The second category of poems included in the anthology comprises poems written either in celebration of an earlier national independence anniversary or contemplatively simply on independence in general. In the former, recollections of the state of affairs in the country during independence anniversary celebrations are captured so that the poems become archival pieces of information on national experience. For instance, Tanure Ojaide's 'Independence Day' written to commemorate the day in 2002. In the poem, Ojaide comments on Gali Umar N'abba and Anyim Pius Anyim's leadership of the two arms of the National Assembly giving crucial information in the national march to now. The poems written about personal anniversaries have varying resonances to the country's independence anniversary and are therefore included in this anthology to share with the reader the poet's critique of the state of affairs as well as their vision or dream for the future. Funso Aiyejina's 'To Abuenameh at five' belongs in this category in its capture of social inequality and the resultant discontent of youth.

There is a third and final category of poems, those which explore themes that are only remotely related or completely unrelated to independence. Interestingly, some of the poems in this category have also been written by elder-statesman poets arguably borne out of a conviction that the national birthday is not a one-day in the year event but one which needs to be constructed and represented as a theme for day-to-day awareness and renewal. The topic of JP Clark's second poem in the anthology 'The Niger Delta' has been at the centre of the Nigerian national question debate for a while.

I shall also point out that a small number of the poems have appeared previously in poetry volumes published by individual writers. Their inclusion in this anthology with the authors' permission is down to the egregious manner in which they handle an issue considered to be extremely significant to Nigeria's identity as a nation.

The opening poem of the anthology 'The traffic then and now' by JP Clark serves as a thread of continuity between the past and contemporary sensibilities in Nigerian society, even though it also contrasts the two periods in national history and experience and has tones of nostalgia in places. The movement signalled in Clark's opening poem is advanced in the second poem 'The fable of This-certain-land' by Olajumoke Verissimo.

In 'Theme of the half-child', Ifowodo explores dialogue in engaging and representing intergenerational differences in perspective on the Nigerian nation. In it the social critic Ifowodo engages Wole Soyinka, another social critic from an older generation, in a conversation about the latter's summation of his post-independence stewards as the 'wasted generation'. The metaphor of the 'half-child' is Ifowodo's descriptor for his own generation whose circumstances he suggested are worse, with bodies and minds trapped in-between freedom and dependency, suppressed by inadequacies induced from a stultifying environment. The choice of the 'half-child' and its link to Soyinka's poetry also exposes an intergenerational trope not uncommon in Nigerian poetry of his generation deeply influenced by earlier ones.

Several poets revisit the Nigerian Civil War (1967–1970), a dark time in national history, and assess its causes and impact. In contrast, while JP Clark's focus on a region rather than nation seems apparent, Uzor Maxim Uzoatu's 'Because of Biafra' is also themed on a region albeit in relation to the nation. The poems account for the plight of segments of the population; those still making penance for Biafra.

Chidi Opara's 'Our journey to here' and Hope Eghagha's 'This marriage' are critical commentaries on Nigeria's inability to attain nationhood or her penchant to destroy the bond between the constituent parts of the union respectively. Both of these poems provide basis and justification for my dismissal of the whole idea of independence anniversary in 'No words, no serenades'. Like many of the poems in the anthology, sarcasm is a powerful tool in commenting not only on the nation but on those celebrity commentators whose remarks are seen now as outdated and ineffective.

In Adebayo Lamikanra's 'Blues for Naija', Independence Day is represented as a time of joylessness, deceit, corruption, poison, ignorance and grieving. Perhaps the poem that most advances hopelessness in the anthology is Femi Oyebode's 'These stunted flowers'. Its last two lines, 'Every straining an echo of the flowers aiming for sight/ But failing, drooping, tethered to the ground stunted', suggest a grim end for the country. But lamentation varies in degrees through the poems in this group and the dimension of pain shifts sometimes. Molara Wood's 'The lost seed' and E.E. Sule's 'Farewell' touch on the brain drain phenomenon and lament the nation's loss to 'faraway lands'. Migration and exile, whether forced or induced, remain a critical element of the Nigerian psyche and linked inextricably to the development questions around nationhood.

Between the poems of hopelessness and those of hope are the poems of supplication, appeals for rain, healing, growth, and prosperity and life. Ismail Bala's 'After the lean harvest, Lord it's time' and Remi Raji's 'Questions and prayers' are illustrative of these. Raji enjoins his readers 'To all the seeds, all the fruits, and all the plants/ and all the trees without names, offer a prayer of rains'.

The sentiments of these poems contrast rather sharply with that in Okinba Launko's 'A song for a mother's birthday' in which Nigeria is preserved as a dream and mother that cannot be polluted. Thus, the poet is able to end on the positive note that it does:

& one day she will heal of her pains
& all will find fulfilment there:
& all will find their fullness there.

This theme of dreams is also explored by Tolu Ogunlesi in 'Nigerian dream' which expresses hope for a new Nigeria in a future generation.

Several poems in the anthology also turn personal tales and experiences into reference points for national stories. In this category are the 'I/We' poems and those in which the poet is a narrator or commentator about a third person. Funso Aiyejina's 'To Abuenemah at five' illustrates the latter while Olu Oguibe's 'All because I loved you' is an example of the former. It is painful in its reflection of the resignation with which many regard the nation after years of youthful anger, frustration and exile. The fact that this poem has ended up in this anthology however is indication that patriots never truly give up on their country. The last two poems of the anthology, Ifi Amadiume's 'Hopefulness' and Tanure Ojaide's 'Harvest song' speak to the volume's overall desire to engage independence and the collective destiny of diverse peoples and create a forum for exploring hope in the future. Although both of these are 'I' poems, their final lines 'the sweet water of hopefulness for the masses' and 'and the harvest song possesses the entire populace' respectively express for the nation as a whole.

—Tope Omoniyi

The traffic then and now

Where fresh and salt waters flow
Each into the other with the tide,
And rain and mangrove forests grow
As neighbours, shaking hands
In winds high and low,
There truly lies the Niger Delta, thousands
Of rivers interweaving their way
Through swamps as a net cast far out into
The sea, none running dry for a day:
This only its dwellers, who have plied
These waters for so long, paddlers with prow
Become a thing of some aura not tied
To time, know deeply to their sorrow.

When oil in the land was of
Another kind, big stern-wheeler boats
Made waves up and down the Niger Delta.
With tall masts, cranes and funnels,
They flew colourful flags, puffing coal
Clouds over forests, full of palm and silk
Cotton trees, jostling *iroko* and mahogany.
Though, with huge hulls and horns,
They often scared canoes off
Their course, the big stern-wheeler boats
Sent siren messages to youths
In towns along the old riverbanks;
And boys, then with no sense of wrong,
On hearing them, rushed the beaches,
And swam out to the ships,
Their crews mainly from upstream,
Offering a hand to pull over gunnels
The few who slipped in the chase.
It was lively fair all the way.

But those old stern-wheeler boats,
With sirens and coal clouds,
Like mist on a river at dawn,
Went away not quite long ago,
When, one night, their owners withdrew,
Not far out of sight, and left behind
Land-lubbers to man old trading posts.
Woken up now by flares and sludge,
Youths with guns, go today for tankers
And anaconda pipelines taking out
The new oil and gas from the same delta.

                                        –JP Clark

The fable of This-certain-land

Once upon a time in This-certain-land
There lived a stream which served a people
Now this stream will not flow its course,
Stumps, rocks, sand, shit, held it in a puddle,
This-certain-land lived on this liquid mess.
For across its borders the world became a village
And as its stench became of global infamy
This-certain-land rose to the status of village fool
And as the moon went in full circle – 50 times
The stream's filth ate up the sun. Dark days
Descended on This-certain-land. As years
Passed, not a soul could be seen to stand
All that was left were a mass of dreamers,
That knew of a famous myth among the Greeks
They left their own gods and sought the Grecians'
They prayed for the twelve labours of Hercules
Soon they too began to dream up a sin for
A man that is a god who would come down
And as Hercules, clean their Augean Stable
But there were too many gods to pray to
For many a man had become a god in the land
And even when they were asked to choose
A god who would help their stream run its course
They hoped that fate would make their choice
For faith was something they carried as burden
They prayed – hoping some god had open ears
So they kept on praying but kept on throwing
More stumps, more rocks, more sand and shit
Into that river which would not flow its course
Their gods – Soponna, Sango, Amadioha and a
Host of others – disowned This-certain-land, and
Relocated from the stench that kills even gods.

—Olajumoke Verissimo

A drunk's sermon at the centenary

Let's remember the noble ancestor today,
      Sir Lugard, a great surgeon;
he who envisioned order
in the tortoise-back mass
of his desire,

mediating the plenary bulk
as an intent closure,
      with overseas-endorsed
measures of narcotics as a retaining wall,
to stem the strewn tides.

You can imagine his eyes growing clearer
      as he contemplated
flippant patterns into the body's slippery
      surrender,
and cast for clarity in the counsel of
home-bound missives.

And remember too, Miss Flora,
      zealous in love,
an eye on a tinker's ethnography,
coalescing the patchwork into
a coastal re-imagining,
      a foreclosure,
mistaken for a love form, to ambiguate
the calculus of a mercantile
episteme....

Let's remember as we dance today,
the elegance of their own departure,
even as the ritual child wobbled
      off the slab,

a protean mutant, alien ribs emerging
on crowded flanks, atavisms,

thought buried deep in the genes
of Enlightenment, imploding, reclaiming
their ancient rebellion…

—Peter Akinlabi

God punish you, Lord Lugard

The traffic warden's white-and-yellow sleeve
stopped our transport, a Lagos mini-bus
bought from one of the rust heaps of Europe –
part of the great scheme to gain reprieve

for the city's long-suffering commuters.
A horde of beggars swarmed the bus; he beat
all to the vantage position in front
of the open door. He had good manners,

and what he lacked, such as the Queen's English,
he faced with uncommon calm and courage;
blind and battered, with a withered left arm,
not for him the plain and unlearned

"Help me for chop, I beg. God go bless you."
Some flourish, or polish, he thought
would persuade far more than suffering's worst gown.
And so he: *"Good day, brodass and sistass".*

"Half massy on me, pliss half sampaty.
Allah's piss for you." In the bus now, silence
and private wars between purse and charity.
"Half ya broda, half sampaty on me."

The conductor, scorning all etiquette
laughed loud, pitying country, not beggar
and swore: *"God punish you, Lord Lugard,*
na you bring this English come Nigeria!"

The white-and-yellow arm beckoned the bus,
a wild fury of horns startled it past
ferrying us beyond claims of charity
and of Lugard's shadow in the black smoke.

— Ogaga Ifowodo

Independence Day

On this Independence Day a woman sack on the head goes
at dawn to her farm unaware of any official proclamations.
She's dependent on her chapped hands and so early leaves
for her self-allotted patch to exercise them for salvation.
Two weeks earlier, also departing at dawn, she escaped
being herded to thumbprint paper for forthcoming elections
that will not put corn, millet, beans, or legumes in her plates—
she has at home still snoring a man, a master that's a pest,
and children she must muster her muscles to make smile!
On bare feet in cotton wear brown from age and sweat
one hand supporting the sagging sack on the head,
she heads for the bush tiring kilometres from home—
today like every day a workday, not a public holiday;
she will not hear the President's national broadcast,
knows not the anthem or flag; knows not Independence.
N'Abba and Anyim don't ring a bell in her bush ears;
she hears not the epic duel between the House and Aso Rock
that threatens the grass under which and for which they fight.
She heads with hoe and machete to celebrate flowering
okro, groundnut, corn, and other edibles hands produce;
she'll drink *sobo*, *burukutu*, and *pito*;
to the music of resident birds happy for human company.
The proclamation partially holds; traffic lighter than usual.
Of the other workers, they must be happy staying at home
no light to watch the television charades of the Government,
the Presidential Message, march-past, parades and all that.
Every day chased out at dawn to the bush for life's sake
on Independence Day the woman sagging sack on her head
takes to the farm, out of town, on her own sovereign mission.

—Tanure Ojaide

No words. No serenades

Golden Jubilee deserves fiestas of jubilation
But emptying the treasury into Eagle Square
Is a sick tale told by rogues to a foolish audience.

Where does one find cerebral words
To serenade a nation at fifty when
Ransom lords ransack a nation in darkness?

Menacing death-traps of potholed roads
Cornerstone of the Minister of Transport's vision
From a harvest of crumpled *Muritalas* into 'polly bags'

Bully cousins in colourful muftis cart away slices
Of national cake in bottomless *Ghana-Must-Go*
Their principals in a paradise tucked into rocks

In half a century, we have grown from crawlers
Straight into crutches. Kainji caged and Cicero
Forever muzzled so river blindness can spread
Our philosophers bury battered dreams and grey

From burying their heads in global sands
Reminiscing about their long gone childhoods
Apprentice dissenters tag along in awe
Pointing fingers away from their festering sore

But we live in a time of higher stakes
So sentences that once stung like 'the man died'
Lie lame today crippled by our feast of polio
Unable to fire the turbines of change

In the jargon of lexical surgeons, authors
Of structures concealing agents of ignoble acts
By foregrounding victimage share in the ignominy
Of the acts they report to the world, lamely.

Yes, we put distance between State House
And Radio House so that inebriated soldiers
On stagger-walk from Steak House no longer wander
On the airwaves to shock a nation only half-awake.

But there's no jubilation for us in Golden Jubilee
No words. No serenades. Just foul-mouthed youths
Groomed to suck their sick nation's tits dry.

—Tope Omoniyi

Our journey to here

We climbed down
From the rickety sea craft
Moored on the sunny mooring.
We,
Happy offspring
Of unleashed giant,
Tethered for decades
In confine of subjugation.
We climbed down
Holding flags
With colours of green and white,
Singing and swaying
To rhythm and rhyme
Of our new anthem,
Investing strength and hope
In our new sea craft,
A craft we will pilot,
We will take
To glorious land of nationhood.
We climbed onto our new craft
And the jostle for captainship began.
In the frenzy
Of our inordinate jostle,
Our sea craft waddled
Through the tempestuous sea.
As we moor
In this middle of nowhere,
To reflect on our journey to here,
Nationhood remains a dream.

—Chidi Anthony Opara

This marriage

When I lugged gourds of palm wine
And tins and tins of hot *ogogoro*
To your father's homestead in Ekrejeta
When I dragged my aged parents with me
To seat with your withered parents in negotiations
Over the curvaceous and oily body of my future wife
Draining my lean purse for the love feast

When I shut my doors to all damsels
Opened my heart to you
Pretty Onome of the slow eyelids
Pretty Onome of the hanging buttocks
Slapping the ambitious daughter of wealthy Kokoricha
In her beautiful oval face
I did not expect a harvest of disappointments
And a bucket of sorrows laced with confusion
In this marriage

After moments of locked tension in years
Issued forth a barrel of bouncing children
Four, then twelve, then nineteen, then thirty six
We sang joyful songs in praise of the Almighty one
We nurtured them in sweat and tears
We tumbled and struggled and fumbled
We built farms and ate yams

Then we fought...

We stood before the magistrate of war
Fighting a bitter divorce matter for three years
The Magistracy was a ding dong
Blood and tears and pogroms and stinking corpses
And fattened vultures later
The fat Pastor's miracle planted another seed

In the vineyard of our marriage

Now in the twilight of my life
When I ought to sit back and drink the palm wine of life
I do not know whether you were my wife of fifty years

Why have we battered
The spirit of this marriage
Like grains in a mortar
After a wrestling encounter with the pounding pestle?
Why?

— Hope Eghagha

Because of Biafra

(To Frederick Forsyth)

We fought the world,
A world that disinherits
Stock damned as original sin
Because of the war on Aburi
We stand sentenced
To pound murky nooks
And hoary chambers
From the gorge of ancestry
In the brood of blood
To the graveyard of the deities,
Shovelling away grains
Gathered with rakes,
Draining source and course
Like spring in retreat,
Upon the drift of dons and dunces
In the solicitous gush
Toward the seraphs of sunset,
Bodying serpentine margins
Of the gulf within
The champion desert
As wasteland works homeland
Baked like scorched earth
By the whiteness of flight
And the blackness of blight.

— Uzor Maxim Uzoatu

Today

This is how you feel on a wind-swept day
You heed the sound of a chain saw from afar off.
You do not hear the trees collapse
The blustery conditions give the budding mango, grapefruit,
guava, pear, papaya trees some playful agitation
The air is fragrant with them all.
You want to inhale and inhale…and inhale
You do not know the species of birds fluttering about in frenzy,
afraid for their homes.
A rake, worked by your father who desires to do these things,
gathers tanned and crispy leaves
You sit in a room of green, also listening to the wind as
she teases the open gate and everything
At your feet are pots of aloe vera and young neem trees
You drink a fat cup of spicy *kunun gyada*
The harmattan murmurs …
It howls from behind the rocks as clan of hyenas would
The old Ford climbs up your red hill grudgingly
The moment; epiphanous
This is how you feel on an unsunny day in October in Jos.
Come on this day, if you ever will.

— Zainabu Jallo

The Niger Delta

Where fresh and salt waters flow
Each into the other with the tide,
And rain and mangrove forests grow
As neighbours, shaking hands
In winds high and low,
There truly lies the Niger Delta, thousands
Of rivers interweaving their way
Through swamps as a net cast far out into
The sea, none running dry for a day:
This only its dwellers, who have plied
These waters for so long paddlers with prow
Become a thing of some aura not tied
To time, know deeply to their sorrow.

—JP Clark

Ships

For the Niger delta

Unseen hands daily smear oil
across the ominous face of the clock,
the gently relentless art of many talented painters.

When that canvas is finished it will harbour
two ships; one sailing into port, loaded
with the symptoms of an oilboom.

The other sailing away, tipping over the edge
of the earth, bearing broken flesh
into an invisible dustbin.

There, and everywhere else, will be blood,
staining the atlas in hues deeper
than the ink that staunchly marks place.

—Tolu Ogunlesi

Where we live

We live here
where love comes
in wrapped words

tongues mumbling
in the belly
of the words

we live in a maze
where razor-in-cheek
cutting through the heart
wastes words
on deaf-dumb...

where wounded words
seized by the jungle
in return for justice
become the ruins
of our lion appetite
living lost dreams
in prodigal measures

yes, we live
        down
                here...

—Sumaila Umaisha

A town I know

There's a town I know
Where all the cabs
Run a one-road route
Past its airport
Up and down
As IBB Way becomes *Eta Gbo*

On all other routes a feast of Okadas
Swell the ranks
Of public transport
Pregnant women and nursing mothers
Balance precariously
Their human luggage
Sandwiched between them
And the pilot cyclist

But the ones that drive my envy
Are the lucky bastards
Who pick up damsels
At the university gate
Their seats slanted to lean
Passengers forward
Raising their backsides
Into place for the imagination
Of rot in bicameral assemblies.

—Tope Omoniyi

Blues for Naija

In this season of joylessness
The rains soak a reluctant earth
Grieving for those labouring in vain
To eke out the little jot of joy
Buried in the agony of numerous wants.

They labour for nothing those who cultivate
The beauty of fertile minds
In a land hollowed out with wants
Of demanding flesh, stripped of the dignity
Of spirits purified by proofing flames.

In the dungeons of rank ignorance
Passions fester in the joy of deceit
Feeding fat on the pus of corruption
As poisons seep unchecked into the soil
To feed the famished spirit of the land.

They lie, those who claim to lead
They cheat, those who make the laws
Injustice sits on the throne of reason
And those who own the blasted land
Have nothing with which to cover their nakedness.

Hope is here burdened with chains
Points of light are smartly snuffed
All around there is the silence of despair
Heads, once proud are bowed in resignation
But the powerful look on askance, resolutely unmoved.

— Adebayo Lamikanra

To Abuenameh at five

This year, your anniversary has been usurped by Mary:
The ebony queen of our nation's five-star Fairyland
Away from the squalor of her neighbouring Maryland
On whose streets our children emptied their discontent
And challenged the billboard slogans of redemption
Held in place by self-loading slow guns of destruction
Deployed as cautionary tales against our future tenses:
Reminders that feast may be prepared in cooking pots
But pots never number among the guests at banquets;
That if ladles fail to divest pots of some of their contents
There are always many willing scrubbers at hand, waiting
To prepare them for a next feast & a next set of guests.

Sure, Mary can afford to be merry in her five-star Fairyland
Far removed from the squalor of her neighbouring Maryland.

Oh riddle, redeem us from the darkness in our blues
Billow forth our sails with a steady hand
To when the Queen of Fairyland becomes herself: a cautionary
tale.

—Funso Aiyejina

Motor park monologue 2

Fallen by gin and smoke
I lie half-asleep
On the fringe of my dreams
Grinning,
Half-dreaming,
My certificates my pillow.
She appears in my half-dream
And frowns at my state.
She died heartbroken
When penury persisted.
Father and mother died,
Siblings also died
Heartbroken.
Children retreated to whence they come.
Hoot of horns rouse me to realism,
Emperor's emissaries enter enclave of hate,
They consort with nihilists
And murder those murdered,
They wound the wounded.
Like bulls enraged
Agberos roam with rage,
"We no go gree" climb to crescendo.

—Chidi Anthony Opara

I sing out of sickness

(For Ebi, after asking: "What makes you write?")

I am sick from chasing robbers that take me for granted
with whips that don't flog and shouts they shut ears from hearing

sick from the lethargic silence of my kinsfolk who suffer
racking pain that doses of pirated Codeine cannot relieve

sick from seeing folks timorous of their endowment
that would enable them smash their scourge and be safe

sick from the blindness of people from under whom lords tap
their wealth and insult them for the misery that breaks the heart.

I am mad at the harrowing hunger churning at them
and cannot go on watching and doing nothing with the pellets

fired at them without provocation as if to tame their restive
stomachs
and children possessed into demons and branded militants;
loathed.

I always chase the lords and their livery of dominion
and only singing without stop provides me respite.

And I throw up at the nauseating body that has become
my land, the once primeval beauty splotched and scarred;

I throw up because I am thirsty in the midst of streams
that flow black pus from poisoned veins now varicose,

dying from sunstroke in the rainforest once a divine canopy
now beheaded by poachers out to choke insatiable sawmills.

And sometimes I am lost in the deep night of my wanderings,
the entire neighbourhood a blackout policed by armed robbers;

then in the pandemonium I look for a way out to be sane
and remain human without humiliating my manhood

especially with drunken soldiers and police on the loose
locking down towns and roads to celebrate their delirium.

Always the orphan gets arrested for killing the sacred cow
and no one who knows the real culprit exonerates the poor one.

Paid party thugs rob the visionary's electoral votes;
pirates highjack the gifted nation's fortune at sea.

Male worshippers gang-rape their goddess
in the belief that her bleeding will flower into billions.

Now victors are condemned to victims,
the wails of the wounded intensify;

tomorrow thieves will be monarchs, governors, and presidents
to the praise chants of ghost writers and red caps.

The world must not crash before holding back harassing hands;
we must not leave it to lightning alone to strike down the
monster.

I run into an unknown landscape a fugitive seeking peace
in a wilderness that harbours hope for the desperate

whose nightmares would light into a refuge of stars
breaking out of nowhere to transform the demons.

This is the life that releases the enchanting songs
that mob my days and nights in a perpetual siege

and I helpless and dazed beyond words of testimony
that get lost before they arrive at their destined end.

I sing out of sickness from multiple afflictions,
sing from the pain of knowledge without memory.

—Tanure Ojaide

Theme of the Half-Child

(Conversation with Soyinka)

I

Ogaga: Now, Sir, no kidding. Wasted, you said,
your generation? Was it bloodshed?

Soyinka: Bloodshed and heartbreak. I was fifty
and had seen the sun whet the misty

morning's boastful hoe. The herdsman's vow
at dawn's light promised the fattest cow.

I had seen the hoe and its glittering blade,
the milking bowls sitting in the shade.

But not the full barn or granary
nor the calf, the beef or the dairy.

Ogaga: And that was all boiled your blood to rage —
thwarted hope against the onrush of age?

Soyinka: Wish it were all, but, no, there was more.
Ah, my fears! I had sensed it long before

they asked me to sing the one-key song of
freedom. I had seen it was not enough

to fold the flag of conquest, raise
the drab banner of victory and cease

to toil or dream. The wounded past,
its grudge fatter, ached to laugh last.

Ogaga: But what god or common good was unserved —
surely, they could dance having fought undeterred?

Soyinka: But not that dance, so brash and wanton!
It called for solemn steps, not drunken

gyrations. Yes, they fought, some of them.
Save a few, they swerved out of tandem

with the total vision. They sat at tea-
tables to break the egg of dreams

truer to the goal. They took count
and led the deep-throated to the fount.

Ogaga: So heartbreak from betrayal. But bloodshed —
wasn't it to keep the sheep in one shed?

Soyinka: So they could be sure of their mutton,
the largest acre for their cotton!

They dug a wide gulf between themselves
and the people. They loaded their shelves

with yams and meat, their banks broke with cash.
Greed bested greed, so the bloody clash

of arms! All who dared the gulf of madness
became fodder or were kept in fetters.

II

Soyinka: Now, come, young man, and tell me. What sorrow
beats your heart with your bones, burns your marrow?

Ogaga: A sorrow greater than yours tenfold!
Remember Tchicaya, sad and bold

with grief, and what he told the wailing Christ?:
"I laugh at your sadness," he said, this heist.

"For your one Judas, I count five on my
fingers!" Yes, Sir, you were pampered. That's why

you were quick to chafe. You saw a promise,
and I? Nightmares and a harvest of plagues.

Soyinka: And that is all — that you have suffered more?
How do you measure pain and keep score?

Ogaga: Certainly not—I am thirty-two
and have never voted! And this too:

that I was born into war, a half-
child, to play with bombs, worse than the calf

littered in a burning bush. You drank milk,
mere water teases my tongue. Soft silk

wrapped your infant skin, I was lucky to find
tattered rags. At my birth, the world had gone blind!

Soyinka: So you envy me? At your age, never
forget, my home was a cage and a fever!

Ogaga: You chose your suffering, because you're a poet!
Like your friend, Okigbo, who saw his death

and beating his gong into a gun went
to meet it! Your generation lent

vigour to the folly that broke your heart.
Mine, banished from the light, ached on the mat

in peace or took its despair to the streets,
stoning the rock where power, stone-deaf, sits.

Soyinka: So what do you desire—what's your prayer?
For it's the same grief, one knitted waste and plunder!

Ogaga: Yes, one grief but grown too large to stay the same,
a cough now tuberculosis, the name

of a worm that bores holes in the lungs and the heart.
I desire this: that the half-child pats

his dying mother's breast and scorn
stillbirth. And my prayer? That the sun

falls from the sky, the sea dry its water
when again reason goes to the slaughter!

—Ogaga Ifowodo

How do we sing a song to fifty years in dependence?

Our life's story plays, miles of twisted reel unfurled
Gold threads on this blood-soaked slippery theatre.
The stage, a sculpted Eternity's crossroads
In shards of palm kernels and cowries engraved,
That spins labyrinths of false exits and entrances.

Moments unformed, unfinished, tattered wraps of our tale unfold
Bearing phantom foetuses in history's dark womb
Seeds of two thousand seasons' wanton rape!
Descendants uncountable, soiled sands on our shores, authoring
multiple texts,
Babel's off-springs, spinners of confused fables.

Our multi-coloured masques dance our dream,
"Ashetani", our tale's hero choreograph the raucous chorus,
Multi-racial hermaphrodite, forked tongue mischief maker,
Imp adorned in many colours, embedded in all creeds
Rainbow-child villain across many worlds.

Steeds of invented history skip across our stage
While our modern choir stutter their song:
"How do we trip a dance to fifty years in dependence?"
Under scions of slavers, thieving leaders, warrant chiefs and
rogue traders
Askaris bedecked in fake medals, tear gas and cattle prods.

Our cast of heroes, villains, spirits and demons,
Narrators who unmake history, defilers of our earth,
Telling tales of the ugly ones, too many so far born,
Plunderers of our collective fortune cursed by deities spurned,
Bankrupt Impresarios in this dim theatre of our betrayal.

Our post-colonial chorus still sputters:
"How do we sing a joyful song to fifty years in dependence?"
Under misleaders that bury live bulls, virgin youth and straying
strangers,

Smashing unformed skulls, sucking black gold blood
In their unholy covenant that is our undying pain

Their abomination our lot condemn to fifty seasons
Of purgatory in wilderness of sorrow and want.
Souls adrift, spirits confounded, nation rudderless
As we await our redemption's prophet – sacrifice
Bearer of our ultimate atonement and emancipation.

Our life story unfinished rocks our theatre,
Foundations quaking, curtains torn, moats cracked
As abused audience become actors taking centre-stage.
For it is our time, we who defy death and claim life
To toss our depraved bloated kings in the lion's ring!

—Tade Akin Aina

The trip

Hua- huaaaaaaaa! Honked the horn
And the rails launched the rolls
Setting out with the rising sun
For Bua; the birth place of bliss

As soon as we gained some speed
A fearsome five hijacked our peace
With faces in masks well hid
Three young men and two brown girls

Ado, Ade, Agu was third
Khadija amd Mary make five
Bandits, armed and looking hard
Blessed with logic, like water in a sieve

Our train
Like goldfish spins in circles
Soulless, beaten, left to ruin
While the spoilers share the spoils.

— Prince Zadok

These stunted flowers

(After Baudelaire)

There was a shadowland once
Between the visible illusion of maps
And the partially immune lair of memory
Perhaps it was a cave, even Plato's subliminal world
Perhaps merely an echo straining to be heard

And the shadowmen, slaves pinioned and tethered
Knew little of light and less of night
Though they lived every breath bathed in darkness
There was a flush of swamp, a corrupting mire
In the inner and psychical delta

Time marched past this latitude
Unfixed, the shadowland drifted like driftwood
What legend stained the corpse of its kings
Lacked for stature and unsung shrivelled further
The shadowmen, slaves pinioned and tethered

In this subliminal world of indiscriminate forms
Blind and ignorant of the sun, of the lunar cycle
Every grasping for knowledge was inchoate
Every straining an echo of the flowers aiming for sight
But failing, drooping, tethered to the ground stunted.

— Femi Oyebode

I am killing this ram for you

I will kneel on its gullet and it will die, no blood spilt
You will enter your husband's house with my blessing
No blood spilt, a life taken without spilt blood
You will be happy, you will have children, you will live long

I can hear the young girls chanting, skins gleaming in the sun
And the ochre is red, red like the evening sun as it sinks
Borne on a barque into the next world
You too will gleam radiant wearing your mother's *ekori*
Your hair, long matted plaits will hang, loaded fruits

Is that not my daughter, that lithe and elegant gazelle?
The fatty omentum is yours and your peers, wear it on your
heads
The hide for your groom to clean and tan and yet yours too
And the meat cleaved and cut to share, all the clan eating and
laughing
Drinking milk, singing, dancing, my lithe and elegant gazelle

Your groom does honour, sitting away hidden from the sun
Tonight we will take you to him, to the hut of pleasure
Will the incense and perfume not call forth his longing?
And your muffled cries, like your mother's, also ecstasy
In another month the ochre will be scraped off to welcome you
home.

—Femi Oyebode

Who am I?

As a tot I was the son of my father
And my clansmen accorded me
The dignities due from ancestral toil
They knew not my destination
But they had vision from my beginnings

When I became a boy
They smiled and complimented
The telling gait of ancestry in my spine
And gallantry in our trademarked walk
In my voice, the pitch of my forebears
Kept the past forever in the present

Now that I am a man, puzzle on their faces
Tell me they no longer know me.
For I am born anew and raised
On elements from too many climes
I have journeyed with the wind
And rode the crest of furious waves
To flirt with flames in distant lands

Even as I carried narratives of my folks
And told tales to strangers about places
And things that are pieces of me
I listened and heard their own tales
Of places and things that are pieces of them
Now I am a confluence of tongues
Merged narratives course through me
As I waltz, salsa and lion-dance in one breadth

The son of my father has become a child
Of a new and perplexed world
New myths, new dreams, new fears
New tongues, new kindred, new homes
Adjust the boundaries of fables and folk tales

New thrills of new threats like models
In computer games, virtual viruses
And half hallucinations of the world
Compressed into a village in my palm

Everything in a giant spin
Everywhere reflections of bits of me
That are pieces of everywhere and everyone
Including you
I am the spin.

—Tope Omoniyi

A song for a mother's birthday

(For Mark Nwagwu)

1.

My country is a dream,
a lovely dream;
they will never change it
to something else —

To me she's always a mother,
so tender I can die for her:
but so many treat her like a whore
& plunder her for their lust

To them she's just a cow, to be
milked till she does expire:
but Nigeria is a home to me:
I will grow my treasures there —

I will grow my treasures there
I will feed her with my dreams

2.

Both in the full & empty time
Or even somewhere in-between,

Amidst the cries of Want & Woe
Which our politicians ignore

I will lend my ears to my country
& make her care for the stricken

In the seasons of plunder or
Cannibal laws — days when Terror

Stalks the streets — I will remain
Faithful by her side, & somehow

Find the petals of a loving kiss
To weave a garland for her

3.

So though our dreams are frequently broken
& leaders betray us, & abandon us, each alone,
To face the raging storms of Life, on our own,

I know it's my country calling me to fight
& not despair, telling me that freedom comes
Only when we win it with Sweat & Blood.

I will feed her with my dreams
I will grow my treasures there

For where else can I go, where the soil & my skin
Can share these same colours so freely?
Where else can I chant my *oriki*, & hear the wind
Respond at once, & with the right tonations?
Where else but in my country, tell me,
Will drums go dizzy in the dance of my lineage?

4.

So both in rain & harmattan haze
Washed in moonlight or the sun's rays

My country will remain a prayer
A song I'll sing every hour

She's a seed I've planted to grow
In the garden we call Tomorrow

My country is the coming harvest
Watered by my tears & my joy

I will dress her in my wishes
I will reap my blessings there

& one day she will heal of her pains
& all will find fulfilment there:
& all will find their fullness there.

—Okinba Launko

Nigerian dream

This sea is the colour of the rainbow
that once stained our skies,
the paintbox from which we splashed
the green and white of the Nigerian Dream.

We twist and turn, gently and merrily
following the paths traced
by sailors more fortunate,
joint seekers of new and elusive dreams.

Soon we shall sight land. No?
We will sink instead, *Titanic*
for the postcolonial age,
our downward dance powered by denial.

'All for all by the magic year';
every year a dream, held together
by webs that continue to live, long
after their spinners have turned to dust.

We will *will* ourselves to stop sinking,
vow to let our pride mark the place
where we refused death by water.
The sea will ignore us; steadily become

The colour of death, the paintbox
from which our children will splash
the faded green, and dirty white,
of the new Nigerian dream.

—Tolu Ogunlesi

Homecoming

Now matters of life to their destinations do draw near
                as look-alike cages to birds receive,
                mankind to rooms & a parlour retreat;
as would an Ohue to his home should forever return
with mind on beaten footpaths, groping on things undone;
                to phone friends about to lose a name,
                for as workers for commerce were famed,
while unfolding yet yearnings of those now here.

Once on a look-alike's sick bed I on the head pry
                as jailbirds to other cells stare
                as look-alike eyeballs in clinics fair.
But oh what groans look-alike tears, what foam and sweat
with half-breath and seas of look-alike promised changes,
                of departing inmates who fret
                about incoming neighbourhood wives,
only to turn away when the heart strays off the bites?

But there is, I say, in this home coming a conscience
                as computer interactive
                programmed to re-sow its captives
where a packed mass as pit latrines to hollowness
must, then, show, whilst for their peace prize to fetch,
                an everlasting life seeker,
                a look-alike babies' playacts
as a remnant, unknown to men, strives for the home-nest.

Still, could it be dreams when our look-alikes fail to change
                from adulterous affairs fun
                in parks as toilets of prayer halls,
from leaving for the village streams and the race is over,
as my home life in earth-ash merged with dust as Nova?
                What crescent lurked across Jerusalem's
                look-alike Rome on to Idunwele,
to roll the tickling clock of everlasting life's shape?

                                        —Omohan Ebhodaghe

Our beautiful game

Today na today! We go deal with dem again
Na home we dey play dem, their own don finish today
We go show dem proper pepper for Stamford Bridge
Smiled the cobbler at the end of the dirty Main Street
A pitiable, almost laughable sight as he speaks
Yet this picture perfect profile of penury beams
The season is ours he sings, as he twiddles his bare feet
A mockery of a dribble, a grin bares his yellow-brown teeth
A feint, a furtive dribbling and his back disappears into an alley
The last I see, the emblazoned 'Essien' on his blue Chelsea jersey

At least he will never walk alone
For at the end of his daily gloom is a golden dome of hope
A galaxy of millionaire maestros' dribble-shooting a football
Soccer gods to adulate when they win, ululate when they fall

But deep in the tunnel of his blues, the swelling at Stamford
Bridge
Lurks the red devil that drowns the new disquiet under Oshodi
Bridge
An arsenal of defty footwork masks the booming guns of the
gunners in our creeks
Suspended animation, suspended nation, suspended people we
no longer speak
Meek Lilliputians, misgoverned, maltreated by misfits
A soothing 'treble' poultice for our engorged blistering woes
The principal balm our roars to the gladiators' goals

Beware, this raging Rooney looney an intoxicating palmy of the
masses
A leveller of the poor, the rich, and all social classes
Lofty goals momentarily forgotten, buried under silverware
Our football ancestors starved, sulking in the cold bosom of our
derelict stadia

Like howling wolves wandering warily across a desolate wasteland

Our local derbies drab, our premier local stadia empty stands

Our ancestors aghast as their offspring now cheering fans of a distant foreign deity

Cheering gustily while the voice of their ancestors fade into the gloom

— Jekwu Ozoemene

All because I loved you

once, i wrote with the irreverence of youth
and the fire of a heart burning to ash
i plucked words like faggots from blazing coal
and on the anvil of exile, i hammered sorrow into verse
the burden of your suffering tore poetry from my flesh
on the night of your hanging, there was dust in my lines
i aimed for song, and not an eye was without tears

i marked the fourteen stations of the cross
but your death has killed my verse
each day, i wake on the hour to mourn
and i feel like a wanderer in a city without lights
passion escapes in the fog and words crumble at my touch
and my throat feels like a concrete floor
the power of tears has deserted me

i walk through the streets of this forbidding town
searching for faces i used to know
and your memory is like a faded picture in the pocket
here and there, i hear your name like the distant crack of a whip
and there is a dull pain where the scars remain
i recall your stubbornness, and the ring of blood on your wrist
and i embrace this cold that severed you from me

once, i howled with the rage of a bard
there was epiphany in the pain
and all because i loved you
now i claw the walls for a naked word
my lines are a hollow sepulchre
ready for the final dust
silence claims us at last

—Olu Oguibe

After the lean harvest, Lord, it's time

After the lean harvest, Lord, it's time
to lay your hands firmer on the hourglass
and in the night let the wild ghosts prowl.

As for the fulsome fruits, hasten them to sweetness.
beam on them three days of gentler wind
to tango them down towards their time, and hound
the final few tinges of brightness through the day.

Whosoever is penniless now, will save no dime;
who lives aloof will live continuously so,
wandering on to write wee, drab oblong poems,
and, along the town's alleys,
ruefully ponder, when the giant gloom retires.

—Ismail Bala

Atop the *NNS Aradu*

Aradu reigns berthed on green brocade as some marine gem

Steady in the laps of Apapa, ropes restraining the power samsonic

Of Nigerian steel. Sea cries silent now, breakwater is an hour passed

Yet I stand alone at top deck — cardinals of the world converge at my head.

My thunder is still but for a while yet I trace the lines, skirt SAMs

And jammers down to the fo'c's'le, intimate cabins where clocks tick still

The sterling friendships of voyage... I wish but to sea again to sea again

To hear the hum and feel the rock of twin diesels proud and strong

For atop the flagship of my country, the navvies of the world part

In hurry and fright for my flag is heir to an ancient black glory, Neptune reborn.

I want to pull away from terrors of senates where my masters trade treacheries

To sea again where there is one story, Nigeria — the Aradu its might and single voice.

— Richard Ali

Questions and prayers

when the locusts come, will you greet them
with tears and blood, in the aftermath of fractured years?

when the termites come with fangs of iron
can you be the grit stubbornness of rocks?

when your throat is filled with fire
why do you watch in silence?

where will you give birth to the red hunger
of truth, who will welcome the sailing tongue?

where will you hide amid these impatient clouds
will you go where the smoke is perfumed light

when your throat is filled with fire?
will you bury the anger in the coffin of laughter?

you are a poet, the incurable child,
can you dream a song for tomorrow?

or are you cursed to cry without ceasing
about wilted seasons fattened in sorrow?

each time you leave you weep
as each time a lover leaves you on a rough road,

each time the wind brings the news of your own bleeding
they ask what will you do, why are you silent as the dead bee?

even if you spit poison as the saliva of oceans
what will happen, what will happen?

still do not sleep, dream but scream at slumber.
will you forget those forgotten in the teeth of dogs

those to whom agony is both foretaste and dessert
whose faces are painted in gloom, who bleed still and dance in
hope?

Salute them all, who never said farewell to our tale.
Salute them, who always return, flowers in the diseased heart.

To all the seeds, all the fruits, and all the plants
and all the trees without names, offer a prayer of rains

—Remi Raji

Stones of heaven

All hail the stones of heaven
Dropping heavily at eleven
In fury...whacking rusted rooftops
A scene to behold as they plummet... ruthlessly ... unforgiving
Upon crop and owner

All hail the stones of heaven
A seraphic throwing contest
You would imagine
At the majesty's decree
Not some magic of meteorology

If only they could be manna
Then we will make a fire
We will dance and not tire
We will learn how to be idle
And how not to be anxious

If only they could be manna
All our energies we shall garner
To erect our store houses
We could put up a banner
And get to truly know our spouses

All hail the stones of heaven
Little glimmering stones
So pure, so potent
Do say: what does the future offer?
What becomes of us?

Do say: what does the future give?
Our souls; shall they stay bare?
Shall we possess our own shadows?
Or remain clustered on a road so narrow
What becomes of our castles in the air?

And like our dreams
You thaw out
Incapable of living out
To cool our racing blood
And the stickiness of our hearts

All hail the stones of heaven
Dropping at eleven
All gone by seven

—Zainabu Jallo

To encircle the land

so much of it comes down to whipping the sponge whipping
the fish.you can play with mastery and revise the tone of the
intrusive doorbell.bind and

unbind.wrap and unwrap.there is something to the black print
of your book.a caress or almost a caress.a grope holding onto its
fidelities.you are always

becoming and always gone.dishes call.lava showers a psalm.
you've come this far for the fruit of your inexorable pariahhood.
from serenity to calamity.

from alterity to a convoy's pause.the floret that begins the movie.
the music of blades.you've come this far insisting on pulsating
duress(as random as

falcon and clover).the way it comes down to shaking up
defamatory syrinxes.what is wrong with being obsessed with the
ridiculous.added to which

there was a yard sale and the chewing of a bouquet.mostly
sinuous and serpentine wish.the purity of debauchery.

—Uche Nduka

True, the sun rises

(Formerly a part of the tradition
of locomotive in pop music)

True, the sun rises but some days
It fails to hitch a ride in a van.
Ignorant of this, the driver fights
Back the sensation of fingers scowling
Over the back of his head.
But the fingers don't belong to the sun.
It's true, the sun has no body.

In one poem, the sun just sails.
In another, it celebrates with what we gained.
But this doesn't concern the sun
Or a driver who feels the fingers' touch.
These fingers, like all fingers,
Belong to the sky, over which
The sun has complete control.

—Ismail Bala

What can I call this?

At the Tee-Junction of decision,
the spot where Ogun's meal
and the acolytes' feet mix
I saw a street like an arrow
and a dream of sparrows and eggs
covered with red camwood
and the richest yellow palm oil
dripping and clinging to Ogun's soil
In the distance I heard a call
sounding like the voice that foiled
Dimka's coup
This is a scared moment
When nothing should move
Not even the rustling leaves
It is a moment when gods in trees
and trees like gods make the present
like dreams and the past a gift
for the memory....
Can we forget the army of change agents
Who are now numbers swollen in the ankle
of our earth?
Who can forget the gallons of blood
that watered deformed democratic plants?
To the distance, with my raw voice
I blessed the winds from the North
And to the East reached for invocations
of rising sun and warrior sons
The waters of the West are calm
But I still need the last psalm
that fights against those after my lamp
There is nothing to mend in the festering South
Those who drill and those who kill

Have joined forces at this tee-junction
of indecision.
They have drilled our land to silly
They have killed our eyes and winners of bread
The street once like an arrow will bend
as they return from the earth that gave them bed

—Kole Ade-Odutola

Farewell

Tight jinxed professors gazing at the immensity of nothing!
Behold a multitude of books speeding away in escape
Pens swagger in hollowness, prostitute with cheap sheets

Afro-haired professors walking the length of the Atlantic in fury!
Bid the sun, bid the moon, bid the stars, bid the rivers
Farewell

Farewell to the flapping bravado of the flag
Farewell to the querulous query of the anthem

Ask the rocks, ask the rivers
ask the ghosts of deserted shelves
ask the rocks, ask the rivers
ask the emasculated walls surrounding shelves

They will be manacled by crooked questions
In their intellection a jeremiad shall burst
They will compose startling rhetoric
Only in amputated tongues!

—E.E. Sule

Travelling

I

My eyes have walked
My eyes have strolled
        On tomorrow's hunches
My eyes see everything in nothing

They say it is the season

Sight speak drought into minds
And hope feels better in purdah
They say it is the season

When the world is battered
And all chatter is of;
Flesh on blood
Blood and bones
Bones in pieces
I pick up my desires and climb out of my heart. I leave.
I go past that place where mothers turned into birds;
Chirp their aches, and eat raw their common silence
It is the season

When women re-imagine cries of dead babies
And hear again the crackle before the crackers
I pick up my desires and climb out of my heart. I leave.
For that place words are spoken into lathered tears
A place where men bath themselves in soaps of ache
I do not know if I will return as I go, but I leave.
I do not know where I go; I'm on my way there
They say it is the season

Stained sculpted water bite into nostrils; stop breath
Fear seize hold of legs, and flesh becomes rock

At this time of trusting evil; craving goodwill
Tears are the same everywhere men are different

This season is hazy and the rains won't stop
I cannot see behind; I imagine what's before me

My heart brims with faith and idle will
The words won't come; there's labial traffic

II

They say it is the season
When words for grief go on strike
And humour takes the place of tears,
Until it gathers us into a laugh

Now, how do I go on to speak my dolour;
Of the to be and the un-be – the mapped livings
Of those things that cringe in corners of my teeth
And turn hate bites and pricks into a daily feast

But what shall I say of this which takes
From me voice and leaves me life?

My eyes have fallen into a dry season.

—Olajumoke Verissimo

The kitchen cabinet coup

The voice was the same
from the station by the grave-yard
the voice without shame
came with the early morning yarn
All soup & kettle pots closed
All beer and brandy bars closed
All 'body-no-be-wood' shacks closed
from dusk till dawn.
Nothing must move till we are done.
Any teeth found masticating
shall be confiscated
any eye ball found roaming
near the Aso throne
will be thrown like a rock
and allowed to rot and roll....
This gourmet is not about rows
We are about war against wars
and war against political whores
who wore their victims like trophies.
These sellers of morphine
when coffins are needed.
these lost hunters who feed
On their dog's entrails.
It is all over,
all over town that intestines
have taken over the Buka
where eaters of the national wealth preside
The restaurants where lickers of leftovers reside
The palace of spittle whose fate dew will decide
The coup was gutless and without gory scenes.
An unknown anthem played on national screens
where martial music once displaced highlife scores.

The coup was salt-less but not flawless
In seasons of low life and 'cough few'
Only fools were caught with third mainland dreams

We are on the march again
To gain freedom from bullet boys,
dressed up in Babanriga
armed with riggers' tools
To dismantle hunger-weaken voice boxes
Watch as a basher comes into view
and all hell will be let loose

A familiar voice all the same,
Far from the station by the grave-yard
This voice without shame
Plays on national memory
"I better be"...dares our votes
I balance budgets like Delta boats
Used to mend broken wedges.
I bribe barrack-boys
I bash bulletin-writers
I...before bombs blast.

—Kole Ade-Odutola

pro-rogue

the rogue is democracy
robed in blue
rogue parliament

in a cornflower coup

he tears up his rouge constitution
ambushes
with statues   speeches   winks

and a resounding slap
between hill and valley
prorogues an echoing cry

cowering
canada's red cheeks bleed
blue

like all cheeks that bleed
without words
wordless

the wife-battering bruise
bled blue oblivion
in the rough small man on the hill
happy as the bluest harp

— Amatoritsero Ede

The lost seed

Mournful, the moon lights
hallowed paths of pilgrims.
They leave their lands to trek
the trail of gold.

Wistful, the wind fans
sand onto faltering feet.
They drag north of the Sahara,
lured by a pitiless mirage.

Somber, the stars blink feebly
on Africa's seed flailing
in torrents that lash
with liquid fury, drowning dreams.

Weary, a tree broods at the root,
clutching at its hollowed womb
its seed driven in gales to seek
faraway lands.

Mournful is the moon
wistful is the wind
somber are the stars.

Few of the seed will return.
The mother tree weeps.

— Molara Wood

Power on the people

Flying on ballots' wings
Sewn by our bleeding fingers
You mouth a new song
From the bowels of the steel house of power
As your praise-singers mock us, and police bayonets poke our
bony behinds
Your fat heels dig deeper into our ribs

Ride higher, fly higher
Your caressing courtiers urge
As our blood flows into muddy gutters…

Eat more, take more
They scream, as the people
Blinded by stinging tears and hunger
Polish your borrowed throne

You are the great baobab
You, the king of lions
Friend of other Lions
Feasting on your kingdom

As we choke on the fumes of power
Our bleeding knees
Crawl over your broken promises
Our lips swollen where your last decree bit us…

O mighty one
Nestled royally in the snake-pit of power…
Can you smell grieving graves?
Will your big ears ever hear
The wailing of starving, dying children?
Strung on betrayed hopes…
The mocking laughter of pot-bellied friends?
Will your eyes ever taste truth?

— Cyril Obi

On a circuit

Herr Leibniz was present
in his shiny automatic Benz; and the chief
warden took us to the public houses:
the bathhouse was full; the warm water
pinched my thighs;

We read tea leaves with the renowned
Author Willie Shakespeare, fresh from his
Year abroad; a long sabbatical spent in Yale
And Harvard: he looked smug that night
At the Nsukka Anthills; his round glasses
Square; the pocket watch proper, he
Wouldn't recognize us anymore, no, not
Without the spyglass, set tamely
To his sight. And we must pass the salt. Pass
The Psalter. Pass the cheese. And pass the
Wine. He no longer whines nor dines over
Gari; he did his hair in the windswept fashion.
Pats his lips nicely with a kerchief,
After every honorary speech –

He choked in his English; shook us to the spine,
With some hint of French accent, learnt
In the cabarets of Nantes; dark –
His fingers, ringed with aquamarine;
Very warm his smirk, rich as chocolate milk –
And a milkweed brunette occupies his time now;
His attention drawn to the flicker of light
From the fireplace; a public herr –
A camera: and an audience –
A humdrum table –
A meeting place –
An occasion to chatter, and to clap,

And snap the neck off a bottled brandy: to
Be the distinguished guest at the high table,
To be dogmatic and scented –
To sound contrived underneath
The stout breasts that beat: to
Stir malely before a dozen cameras –

We dined later that night,
At the Drowning Fish by the lagoon;
There were poets and painters,
And a few journalists in town –
A fourteen carat barmaid, ushered
Us in, chaffered the lamb to a malady:
From the depths of a wine bottle,
Zik's library seemed gaunt, dusty
From the Harmattan wind at dusk:
O love! What a shame –
What a lovely shame & a banquet –
The buffet grew cold, over the lethargic crowd
Milling to see Ben Enwonwu, lying-in-state
In the gallery; on the caramel wall – the looming deity
In pure charcoal and pastel gawks at the tenement
Of cabinet ministers, sole proprietors, collectors of fine art:
Lord, I have loved them all: I have tasted the rich bile of
Their laughter: I passed my hand under the moon glow
Into a sister's pine grove – the looming deity gawked,
Winked and remained still: what a fine job, lovely,
What favourable day of the week; and I, your jiggling –
Stalk the fierce night until she wakes.

—Obi Nwakanma

Wonderland

My eyes have seen a mystery dog
Gorgeously dressed like a Lagos queen
The dog was clad in *aso ofi*
A fat necklace that shined like gold
In its right hand a pleasure bag
Swinging and swinging its hip
As it marched down, down the village path.

As I descended the hills of *eemo*
Just bursting out of the lane to *menumo*
I met a goat that permed its hair
And I saw a sheep that permed its hair
Their hairdresser was a corporate pig.

But how come that the Purdah of the Year is a cat to the core?
Her husband, a sheikh,
A chartered merchant of roasted pork
The pastor of this house is a cat to the core
He is the vigilant metaphor of an aged fox.
For just within a week of a special vigil
He planted a bomb in a sister's womb.

In this our land of transition
Whoever says that death is not on course?
This our college of a demon's craze
Where the teacher is daft like an ass
Where the driver is blind like a bat
And the collector calling passengers into the smoking train
He is a chronic sta-sta-stammerer from his mother's womb.

Our Minister for Water is a doctor of death:
He manufactures menopause into the public tap
On blessed day of faltering flow
The tap is a colourful den of typhoid pest.

In the heart of a swindled paradise
Arrows and spears are dancing in macabre spree
But how can sanity return to my bosom land
When the justice of peace is lost in an Arabian fable
Whoever will heal the ailing multitude
Now that the king resides in Ambulance Rock?

— Akeem Lasisi

Friday night live

Our dreams are hindsights,
travelling to the people under the earth,
journeying down the cities,
filling the centuries with sons
so fat they can't pass the needle's eye.

Only the ointment keeps faith,
in the hands of a daughter,
preparing you for burial,
the unleavened bread
calls forth mourners

and prostitutes eating bread
with hallowed hands.
Henna mingles with tears
at the eleventh hour when
rejected pebbles fall like death
sentences on brown earth

This wine sets my eyes
to still waters on barren hillsides.
This wine red in the cup.
The Scarlet thread.
The broken donkey.
Linen breeches dyed in crimson.

The air is rich in prophecies and revolutions.
Within the olive tree, a
copulation is aflame,
burning the bush full of grass widows.
The light shimmers upon the waters.

Light is a quiver of arrows.
Light is an earthquake.
Light is a stormy wind.

Light is a great cry,
electric on bones and skulls.

The bones are diving for flesh.
The shrouds are dying in the stars,
there is light in our loins.

—Toyin Adewale-Gabriel

I am a million selves

I am the million selves speaking silently to the strange winds
of my country of urgent memoirs, …

I am the cactus tree, bearing your names on my bark
I am the sudden breath of the hurricane,

And I am the meaning of your survival, beyond Sorrow's
symphony
I am the drowning man, the snake may just be my redemptive
rope

I am the rough sweet tongue of the city scoundrel
bonded to the beauty and the sclerosis of violent syllables

I drink the sweltering air, the rapid rain, the sizzling sun
And I, the fever on the lips of fattened cowards

I sing about the sins of the flock and the cleric's scars
So what if these priests pronounce the order of the damned

I am the desires of the hungry fly and the owner of sores
Civil cannibals both, they will eat each other before a quarrel

I am the piecemeal deaths you see on the streets
The many meagre debts wrapped as knots in your daily meal

I am the competence and the hypocrisy of guile
the bruise and the blood from this stone of a country.

—Remi Raji

The interview

The silence fills up with her absence.
We hope it speaks our difference.
We feel special, guardians of good practice,
watchmen of the word. The hired hellos
smile when we scowl. Paid to wait,
they will go when she comes.

We know there is a world that will pay
for her ear wax, and queue to see her
stretching like a sentence out of touch
with meaning and beginning. They don't care
she is not the writer of her books.

We came prepared, doing drills, but
this is major league, and I am the rookie:
Whatever happens, avoid her eyes.
Imagine her curls as snakes.
She is Medusa with a fish tail.
One look, you are gone.
He knows her, knows himself.
Their second meeting.
She killed him the first time.

We still our thoughts and wait. And wait.
Then the best-selling body of the moment
arrives, trailing fragrance, prints herself
with hugs that last, spreading a smile
of promise and mystery. I think
of the Da Vinci woman and burn.
Beside me he stares, still as stone.
She has killed him again.

– Afam Akeh

Bag lady

I

Bag lady with sackfuls of regret
Rolled in a knapsack, heaved, hauled
As the mollusc bears around its home.

She moves as with feelers, unseeing
Eyes in rituals of avoidance, noses up
Repelled by a sight they would not see.

Woman to whom things have been done
Sacrificial wearer of scars, bearer of losses
Walking wounded from battles long lost.

II

Bag lady with sackfuls of regret
Tucked deep in under-eye pouches
Stuffed down the protuberant tum.

Beaten to a pulp by life's fictions
Hers is the joy of a wandering haze
A happy face on life's sad street.

She walks, magnificent as Monroe
Dark as Alek, regal as Iman – owning
Nothing, she claims ownership still.

At peace with her many loads, knowing
If you must own nothing, own your regrets.

— Molara Wood

Hopefulness

(After "Bitter" in *Passion Waves*, 1985)

A rapper in stomping words tells me,
as you live life, you live and learn!

I am fully steeped in learning, I tell me!
The Niger Delta still burns spewing black oil,
polluting the waters, the land, the air, the sky.
Only men still rule, I mean at the top-est,
maybe not just in black ties,
deliberately exhibiting much needed Africanness,
insincerely wearing adires, boubous, danchikis, up and down.
Women still spread tender leaves of green bitterleaf
on hand-woven mats spread out in the open,
slowly drying under the blazing sun.
You see, we are still taking the bitter with the sweet,
my other way of talking about the living and learning of life.

A rapper in stomping words tells me,
as you live life, you live and learn!

I am fully steeped in learning, I tell me!
I see also other green leaves
beyond this side of the tropical sun.
An interactant, a traverser, I live and learn
I am the assertive masses who dream
of the sweetness of water
after a meal of bitterleaf soup.
I am also the interactive masses
throwing paper planes all over these shores and beyond,
across the Mediterranean Sea to the masses above,
Paper planes across the Atlantic Ocean to all the Africans there,
Paper planes across the Indian Ocean to the African masses,

Paper planes far beyond the Pacific Ocean to all the world, Africa-born.

A rapper in stomping words tells me,
as you live life, you live and learn!

I am fully steeped in learning, I tell me!
Now that I have again put my foot in with the masses
far beyond these vast seas and oceans of diverse peoples,
gladly sharing meals with the masses everywhere,
I am eating African greens, *kalalu, ewedu, ugbogolu, gbologi!*
I am tasting the sweetness of love, friendship and struggle!
I know another kind of the sweetness of water
after a meal of bitterleaf soup;
the sweet water of hopefulness for the masses.

— Ifi Amadiume

Harvest song

Eagles fly high but they tell me this one won't soar,
since it's Nigerian-bound; they mock human intelligence.
Birds sing, but they tell me our chorus on wings is dumb
because, of course, Nigerian; they ridicule our birthright.

I go to bed to work hard; I accomplish in a few hours
what they swear will never come true in a lifetime.
I plant in the reviled soil and the crops grow abundantly,
and the harvest song possesses the entire populace.

—Tanure Ojaide

Contributors

Sulaiman Adebowale is the Director of Amalion Publishing based in Dakar, Senegal. He was Managing Editor at the Council for the Development of Social Science Research in Africa (CODESRIA), Dakar, Senegal and Editor at the Bellagio Publishing Network in Oxford, UK, a network of publishers to promote publishing in Africa and the South. He has worked as a print journalist and consultant editor for several organizations. He studied English at the University of Lagos, Nigeria and publishing and electronic media at the International Centre for Publishing Studies, Oxford Brookes, UK.

Kole Ade-Odutola is a teacher, poet, photojournalist and activist. Kole trained first as a botanist, earning a bachelor of science degree, with specialisation in environmental ecology and genetics in 1984 from the University of Benin, Nigeria. In 1998, Kole received a master's degree in TV/Video for Development from the University of Reading (UK) on a British Council Chevening scholarship. On relocating to the United States, he earned another master's degree in Organisational Communication at Ithaca College. His collection of poetry, *The Poets Fled*, was published in 1992. His second, *The Poet Bled (1998)*, is dedicated to Ken Saro Wiwa, the author and environmental activist who was killed in 1995 by the Nigerian military junta. His poetry has also been featured in publications, literacy magazines, and journals. He is the author of *Diaspora and Imagined Nationality: USA-Africa dialogue and cyberframing Nigerian nationhood* (Carolina Academy Press, 2012).

Toyin Adewale-Gabriel is a poet, short fiction writer, literary critic and editor. She obtained an MA in Literature in English from Obafemi Awolowo University, Ile-Ife, Nigeria and pursued a career in copywriting for leading advertising agencies in Nigeria including Oglivy, Benson and Mather, and STB-McCann. Her publications include: *Naked Testimonies* (1995); *Die Aromaforscherin* (1998); and *Flackernde Kerzen* (1999). She co-edited *Breaking the Silence* (1996) and edited *25 New Nigerian Poets* (2000) and *16 Nigerian Women Short Stories* (2005). She is poetry editor of Nigeria's *Times Review of Arts and Ideas* and Chairperson of the Women Writers Committee of PEN Nigeria.

Richard Ali is a lawyer and publisher based in Abuja, Nigeria. He is the Editor of the online Sentinel Nigeria magazine and runs Parrésia Publishers Ltd – home to Helon Habila, Abubakar Adam Ibrahim, Chika Unigwe amongst others. He is the author of the novel *City of*

Memories (Parrésia, 2012) and a forthcoming début collection of poems, *Flower in the Sun*.

Afam Akeh is an award-winning poet, literary editor and graduate of the University of Ibadan, Nigeria. He was the Editor of the Times Literary Supplement of the Nigerian *Daily Times in the early 1990s* and founding editor of *African Writing Online*. His works have appeared in *Fate of Vultures and Other Poems* edited by Musaemura Zimunya, Peter Porter and Kofi Anyidoho (Heinemann-BBC, 1990), *Camouflage: Best of Contemporary Writing from Nigeria* (Treasure Books, 2006), *Voices from the Fringe* (ANA, 1988) and in reviews such as *Londonart, Sentinel Poetry Magazine* and *Maple Tree Literary Supplement*. He is the author of *Stolen Moments* (Malthouse Press, 1988) and *Letter Home and Biafra Nights* (SPM Publications, 2012). He is currently Director at the Centre for African Poetry, at www.centreforafricanpoetry.org.

Ifi Amadiume is Professor of Religion and African Studies at Dartmouth College, USA. She has taught at the University of Nigeria, and the School of Oriental and African Studies, United Kingdom; and has written many essays and books with special interest in gender analysis. Her publications include *Male Daughters, Female Husbands: Gender and Sex in an African Society* (Zed Books, 1987); *African Matriarchal Foundations: The Igbo Case* (Karnak House, 1987); *Reinventing Africa: Matriarchy, Religion and Culture* (Zed Books, 1997); and *Daughters of the Goddess, Daughters of Imperialism* (Zed Books, 2000). She has published three award-winning poetry books: *Passion Waves* (Karnak House, 1985, winner of a Commonwealth Poetry Prize nomination); *Ecstasy* (Longman Nigeria, 1995, winner of the Association of Nigerian Authors 1992 Cadbury Literary Award for Poetry); *Circles of Love* (Africa World Press, 2006, and, *Voices Draped in Black* (Africa World Press, 2007). Amadiume's poems deal with love of people, nature, Sufism and struggle, and celebrate activism and activists.

Tade Akin Aina is Program Director, Higher Education and Libraries at Carnegie Corporation of New York. He was Regional Representative for East Africa, Ford Foundation and Deputy Executive Secretary at the Dakar-based Council for the Development of Social Science Research in Africa (CODESRIA). Aina taught urban poverty, governance and development at the University of Lagos from 1980–1993. His most recent publication is *Giving to Help, Helping to Give: The Context and Politics of African Philanthropy* co-edited with Bhekinkosi Moyo (Amalion, 2013). He is completing a collection of poetry for publication.

Peter Akinlabi holds a BA in English from the University of Ibadan and an MA in English and Literary Studies from the University of Ilorin, Nigeria. His poetry has been published in the *Maple Tree Literary Supplement* and *Sentinel Literary Quarterly* where is poem 'Moving' won the First Prize in the Sentinel Literary Quarterly Poetry Competition in 2009.

Funso Aiyejina is Professor of Literatures in English, Department of Liberal Arts, the University of the West Indies, St. Augustine, Trinidad and Tobago. He has published short stories, poetry, and articles and reviews on African and West Indian literature, and his radio plays have been broadcast in Bonn, Ibadan, Lagos, and London. He is the author of *The Legend of the Rockhills and Other Stories* (Tsar Books, 2000), winner of the Commonwealth Writers' Prize for the Africa region in 2000. His first collection of poetry *A Letter to Lynda and Other Poems*, won the ANA Prize in 1989.

Ismail Bala teaches at the Department of English and French, Bayero University, Kano, Nigeria. In addition to his many academic publications, his poetry and translations have appeared in journals such as *Poetry Review, Ambit, New Coin, Okike,* and *A Review of International English Literature.* He has also co-edited a number of anthologies, including *Pyramids: An Anthology of Poems from Northern Nigeria* (2008) with Ahmed Maiwada, *Fireflies: An Anthology of New Nigerian Poetry* (2009), and *Crumbled Spell: Association of Nigerian Authors Anthology of Poetry* (2010). He is an alumnus of the Iowa Writing Program.

John Pepper Clark, also known as JP Clark-Bekederemo studied English at the University of Ibadan, where he founded *The Horn*, a magazine of student poetry. After graduating with a degree in English in 1960, he began his career as a government information officer and then as the features and editorial writer for the *Daily Express* in Lagos (1960–62). A year's study at Princeton University on a foundation grant resulted in his *America, Their America* (1964). After a year's research at Ibadan's Institute of African Studies, he became a lecturer in English at the University of Lagos and coeditor of the literary journal *Black Orpheus.* Clark's collected verse include *Poems* (1962), *A Reed in the Tide* (1965), *Casualties: Poems 1966–68* (1970), *A Decade of Tongues* (1981), *State of the Union* (1985, as JP Clark-Bekederemo), and *Mandela and Other Poems* (1988). His first three plays (published together under the title *Three Plays* in 1964) are *Song of a Goat* (performed 1961), *The Masquerade* (performed 1965) and *The Raft* (performed 1978). He also wrote *Ozidi* (performed in the early 1960s; pub. 1966), and also produced a film (with Francis Speed; *The Ozidi of Atazi* [1972]).

Omohan Ebhodaghe attended the universities of Benin and Lagos in Nigeria. He was the former publicity secretary of the Association of Nigerian Authors, Lagos state chapter. In 1993, he co-edited an anthology of poems and stories entitled *Twenty Nigerian Writers: Portraits* co-edited with Victor Ayedun-Aluma (ANA, 1993), *Hightower: Ibhayu Poetry* (Africa World Press, 2007), and a novel, *In the Midst of Loafers* (Chipmunka, 2011).

Amatoritsero Ede is an award-winning poet and the publisher and managing editor of *Maple Tree Literary Supplement, MTLS* and doctoral candidate in English literature at Carleton University, Canada. His first collection of poems, *Collected Poems: A Writer's Pains & Caribbean Blues* (Yeti Press, 1998) won the ANA All Africa Christopher Okigbo Prize for Literature followed by his second collection, *Globetrotter & Hitler's Children* (Akashic Books, 2009). His works have appeared in several anthologies: *TOK 1: Writing the New Toronto* edited by Helen Walsh (Zephyr Press, 2006), *Camouflage: Best of Contemporary Nigerian Writing* edited by Nduka Otiono & Diego Okonyedo (Treasure Books, 2006), *May Ayim Award Anthology* edited by Peggy Piesche et al. (Orlanda Verlag, 2004), *The Fate of Vultures: BBC Prize-Winning Poetry*, Peter Porter et al. eds. *(Heinemann, 1989), Und auf den Strassen eine Pest,* Uche Nduka ed. (Horlemann Verlag, 1996) and *Voices from the Fringe: An ANA Anthology of New Nigerian Poetry,* Harry Garuba ed. (Malthouse Press, 1988). He edited *Sentinel Online* poetry journal from 2005 to 2007.

Hope Eghagha is a poet, novelist, playwright and senior lecturer in the Department of English, University of Lagos. He was a member of *The Guardian* (Lagos) Newspaper Editorial Board. A graduate of Theatre Arts, University of Jos, Nigeria, Eghagha has so far published a play *Death, Not a Redeemer* in 1998 and four collections of poetry: *Rhythm of the Last Testament, This Story Must Not Be Told, The Governor's Lodge,* and *Premonitions and Other Dreams,* and a novel, *Emperors of Salvation.* He is the Commissioner for Higher Education in the government of Delta State, Nigeria.

Ogaga Ifowodo is a lawyer, human rights activist and poet. He taught poetry, creative writing and literature at Texas State University-San Marcos, USA. He has an MFA and PhD from Cornell University, USA. He has published three collections of poems, *The Oil Lamp* (Africa World Press, 2005), *Madiba* (Africa World Press, 2003), *Homeland and*

Other Poems (Kraft Books, 1998). He has won several international awards for his poetry. He was detained between 1997 and 1998 by the military regime of General Sani Abacha, an experience which formed part of the story 'The Travel Commissar'.

Playwright and poet, **Zainabu Jallo's** play *Onions Make Us Cry* was short-listed for the NLNG Literary Prize 2010, and was one of the winning plays of the National Studio London Africa project. Her other plays, include *Holy Night, Caught in the Blank, My Sultan Is a Rockstar, These Feelings, The Revolutionary Carrot* and *High on Eleven*. She has been an international residency fellow at the Royal Court Theatre, UK; the Global Arts Village, Delhi, India; Château de Lavigny, Maison d'écrivains Fondation Ledig-Rowohlt, Lausanne, Switzerland; the Instituto Volusiano de Artes in Sao Paulo, Brazil; and at the Sundance Theatre Lab, USA.

Adebayo Lamikanra is professor of pharmaceutical microbiology at the Obafemi Awolowo University, Ile-Ife, Nigeria. In addition to numerous academic publications, Lamikanra is the author of *Wake Me Up in the Year 2000* (1994) and *Under the Almond Trees* (Collection of Essays, 1996). *The Lean Years (1997), Heart Sounds* (Kraft Books, 2000), a collection of short stories *A Round Half-Dozen* (Kraft Books, 2002), and *Essential Microbiology* (2010).

Akeem Lasisi is an award-winning journalist, author and performing poet known for his experimentations with oral Yoruba and English poetry. Lasisi's first published work, *Iremoje: Ritual Poetry for Ken Saro-Wiwa*, won the Association of Nigerian Authors (ANA/Cadbury) Poetry Prize in 2000, and the second, *Wonderland*, was runner-up for the same prize in 2001, and *Ekun Iyawo: The Bride's Chant*. Lasisi holds an MA in Literature from the University of Lagos, Nigeria. After teaching English language and literature in secondary schools, he moved to journalism, working as a proof reader, production sub-editor and arts and features writer. Presently staff writer with *TEMPO* Magazine, whilst still maintaining his poetry performing outfit.

Okinba Launko is a pen name of the playwright, poet, theatre director, university professor, and literary theorist, Femi Osofisan. Among his literary awards and commendations are prizes from the Association of Nigerian Authors (ANA) for both drama (1980) and poetry (1989), the Folon-Nichols Award from the African Literature Association and in 2004 he was awarded the Nigerian National Order of Merit (NNOM), the nation's highest academic recognition. Among his numerous works include *Kolera Kolej* (1975), *Who Is Afraid of Tai*

Solarin (Scholars Press, 1978), *Birthdays Are Not for Dying and Other Plays* (Malthouse Press, 1990), *Esu and the Vagabond Minstrels* (New Horn, 1991), and *The Women of Owu* (Ibadan Univ. Press, 2006). His poems include *Minted Coins* (1987), *Cordelia* (1989) and *Dream-Seeker on a Divining Chain* (Kraft Books, 1993). He was educated at universities of Ibadan, Dakar, and Paris.

Uche Nduka was born (1963) and raised in Nigeria. His books include *Flower Child* (1988), *Second Act* (1994), *The Bremen Poems* (1995), *Chiaroscuro* (which won the Association of Nigerian Authors Prize for Poetry in 1997), *Belltime Letters* (2000), *If Only the Night* (2002), *Heart's Field* (2005), *eel on reef* (2007), *Tracers* (2010) and *Nine East* (2013). Poet, lyricist, photographer, essayist, he currently lives and works in Brooklyn, New York.

Obi Nwakanma is a poet, journalist, biographer, literary critic, and Assistant Professor in the Department of English, University of Central Florida, USA. Nwakanma's first collection of poems, *The Roped Urn*, was awarded the Cadbury Prize in 1996 by the Association of Nigerian Authors. *Thirsting for Sunlight*, his biography of the modernist poet, Christopher Okigbo, was published by James Currey in 2010. His second collection of poems, *The Horsemen & Other Poems*, was published by Africa World Press in 2007. He received the Walter J. Ong Award for Distinguished Achievement in 2008 from Saint Louis University, USA. His poetry, fiction and essays have appeared in various anthologies and publications including *Okike, Vanguard Review, Callaloo,* and *Wasafiri*. Obi Nwakanma has also worked as a professional journalist, reporting internationally for *Newsweek, Neue Zurcher Zeitung,* and as literary editor for the *Vanguard,* Nigeria, for which he continues to write a weekly column, 'The Orbit' in the *Sunday Vanguard.*

Cyril Obi is currently a Program Director at the Social Science Research Council (SSRC) and leads the African Peacebuilding Network (APN) program, in New York, USA. From January 2005–2011 he was a Senior Researcher at the Nordic Africa Institute (NAI) in Uppsala, Sweden. Dr. Obi is also a Research Associate to the Department of Political Sciences, University of Pretoria, South Africa, and a Visiting Scholar to the Institute of African Studies, Columbia University, New York.

Olu Oguibe is currently Professor of art and art history at the University of Connecticut, USA. His published collections of poetry include *A Song from Exile, A Gathering Fear* which won the Christopher Okigbo All Africa Prize in 1992, and *Songs for Catalina*. Oguibe is a recipient of many awards, among them the Connecticut State Governor's award for lifetime achievement in the arts.

Tolu Ogunlesi published his first poetry collection, *Listen to the Geckos Singing to a Balcony* (Bewrite Books, 2003), while still pursuing his pharmacy degree. His novella for young adults, *Conquest and Conviviality* (Hodder Murray) was published in 2008. Ogunlesi's poetry has appeared in *The Lagos Review*, *Wasafiri*, *Sable*, *Daily Times*, *The London Magazine*, *Stanford Magma*, *Stanford's Black Arts Quarterly* and *World Literature Today*, amongst others. His journalism has appeared in the London *Independent*, *Huffington Post*, CNN.com, *Caravan* and *NEXT*. He has received a number of awards including the Dorothy Sargent Rosenberg poetry prize 2007, Nordic Africa Institute Guest Writer Fellowship in 2008, and the Cadbury Visiting Fellowship by the University of Birmingham in 2009. He graduated from the Creative Writing programme at the University of East Anglia, UK.

Tanure Ojaide is the Frank Porter Graham Distinguished Professor of Africana Studies at the University of North Carolina at Charlotte, USA and a leading poet, essayist and novelist. He has won major national and international poetry awards, including the Commonwealth Poetry Prize for the Africa Region (1987), the BBC Arts and Africa Poetry Award (1988), the All-Africa Okigbo Prize for Poetry (1988 and 1997), and also the Association of Nigerian Authors' Poetry Prize (1988 and 1994). Tanure Ojaide's sixteen poetry collections include *Labyrinths of the Delta* (1986), *The Fate of Vultures* (1990), *The Blood of Peace* (1991), Daydreams of Ants (1997), *Invoking the Warrior Spirit: New and Selected Poems* (1999), *In the Kingdom of Songs: A Trilogy* (2002), *I Want to Dance & Other Poems* (2003), *The Tale of the Harmattan* (2007), *Waiting for the Hatching of a Cockerel* (2008), and *The Beauty I Have Seen* (2010). His other writings are: a memoir, *Great Boys: An African Childhood* (1998); two collections of short stories titled *God's Medicine Men & Other Stories* (2004) and *The Debt-Collector and Other Stories* (2009); three novels, *Sovereign Body* (2004), *The Activist* (2006), and *Matters of the Moment* (2009); and six books of literary criticism.

Tope Omoniyi is Professor of Sociolinguistics at Roehampton University, UK. He has taught and held academic research positions in three continents: Africa, Asia and Europe during the last two decades. He is the author of a volume of poems, *Farting Presidents & Other Poems* (Kraft Books, 2001), contributor to six Forward Press anthologies, and to poetry magazines in Malaysia, Nigeria, Singapore, UK and the USA. His academic publications include *Contending with Globalisation in*

World Englishes, co-edited with Mukul Saxena (Multilingual Matters, 2010), *The Sociology of Language and Religion: Change, Conflict and Accommodation* (ed.) (Palgrave Macmillan, 2010), *The Sociolinguistics of Identity,* co-edited with Goodith White (Continuum, 2008), *Cultures of Economic Migration,* co-edited with Suman Gupta (Ashgate, 2007), *Explorations in the Sociology of Language and Religion,* co-edited with Joshua A. Fishman (John Benjamins, 2006), *Nigeria and Globalization: Discourses on Identity Politics and Social Conflict,* co-edited with Duro Oni, et al. (CBAAC, 2004). and *The Sociolinguistics of Borderland: Two Nations, One Community* (Africa World Press, 2004).

Chidi Anthony Opara is the publisher and editor-in chief of Chidi Opara Reports, a news blog published by the non-profit PublicInformationProjects. He has published several collections of poems *Homeland Melodies and Other Poems* (2008), *Moonlight Monologue and Other Poems* (2009), *Mundane Musing and Other Poems* (2011), *State of Di Nation and Other Poem Dem* (2012).

Femi Oyebode is a medical doctor and Professor of Psychiatry, National Centre for Mental Health, University of Birmingham, UK. His writings include *Naked to Your Softness and Other Dreams* (1989), *Indigo Camwood and Mahogany Red* (1998), *Selected Poems* (2003), *Madness at the Theatre* (2012) among others.

Jekwu Ozoemene is a banker, poet and playwright. He holds a BA in English from the University of Lagos, Nigeria, an MBA in Finance from the University of Leicester, UK and is currently a doctoral candidate at the University of Zambia. He is the author of *Shadows of Existence: An Anthology of Poetry* in 2009, and a collection *The Anger of Unfulfillment: Three Plays Out of Nigeria* in 2011.

Remi Raji is the pen name of Aderemi Raji-Oyelade. He has won national and international recognition for his writing. His volumes of poetry include *A Harvest of Laughters* (1997), *Webs of Remembrance* (2001), *Shuttlesongs America: A Poetic Guided Tour* (2003), and *Lovesong for my Wasteland* (2005). Remi's works have been translated into French, German, Ukranian, Swedish, and Catalan. He was a Research Fellow at the Centre of African Studies, Cambridge University, he is an associate professor at the University of Ibadan, Nigeria.

E. E. Sule is the pen-name for Sule E. Egya, associate professor in the Department of Languages and Linguistics, IBB University, Lapai, Nigeria. He taught Creative Writing, African Literature and Modern Literary Theory in the Department of English & Literary Studies,

University of Abuja, Nigeria. He is the author of two collections of short stories *Impotent Heavens* and *Dream and Shame*; and three volumes of poetry, *Naked Sun, Knifing Tongues* and *What the Sea Told Me*. His novel *Sterile Sky* (2012) won the Commonwealth Writers Prize Africa Region in 2013.

Uzor Maxim Uzoatu directed his first play *Doctor of Football* in 1979. He was the 1989 Distinguished Visitor at The Graduate School of Journalism, University of Western Ontario, Canada. He is the author of 'Satan's Story', 'A Play of Ghosts', 'The Missing Link', nominated for the Caine Prize for African Writing, 'God of Poetry' and 'Cemetery of Life'. He is currently writing the text for photographer Owen Logan's caricature of Michael Jackson in a Nigerian adventure entitled 'Masquerade'. He was educated at universities in Ife and Lagos.

Sumaila Umaisha is the Literary Editor of *New Nigerian* Newspapers, Kaduna, Nigeria. He is a two-time winner of Literary Journalist of the Year Award by the Association of Nigerian Authors.

Olajumoke Verissimo's first book *I Am Memory* (Dada Books, 2008) won two national awards and received an honourable mention from the Association of Nigerian Authors. She has an MA in African Studies from the University of Ibadan and BA in Literature in English from Lagos State University, Nigeria. She is a recipient of the Chinua Achebe Centre Fellowship. Her works have appeared in several anthologies including *Migrations* (Afro-Italian) edited by Wole Soyinka (Voldposten, 2010), Livre d'or de Struga (*Poètes du monde,* sponsored by UNESCO) and many others.

Molara Wood is the former arts and culture editor of *NEXT*. Her work has been published in journals and anthologies, including *African Literature Today, Sable Litmag, A World of Our Own* (FEMRITE, Uganda), *Dream Chasers* (Nelson, Nigeria), *One World* (New Internationalist, 2009) and *A Life in Full* (2010 Caine Prize Anthology). She is the author of *Indigo*, a collection of short stories.

Prince Abiathar Zadok is a composer, poet, playwright and short-story writer. He is the Coordinating Producer of African Theatre Development Foundation, an outfit dedicated to the preservation of traditional African theatre. His published collections of poems include *Sunrise, Mosoto: The Season of Love, We Shall be There,* and *The Child Must Die*. Some of his plays include *Hell Is a Woman, Nzeanzo: The Enigma, The Conquest of Death* and *The Wedding*.